AF539894

ADJUSTMENT OF PROSPECTIVE TEACHERS

ADJUSTMENT OF PROSPECTIVE TEACHERS

By

Dr. T.J. Mounisuvarna Raju

Dr. S.N. Rao

Deptt. of Training, Devt. & Education
English & Foreign Languages University
Tarnaka
Hyderabad

&

Dr. T. Sharon Raju

Assistant Professor
Deptt. of IASE
Andhra University
Visakhapatnam

DISCOVERY PUBLISHING HOUSE PVT. LTD.
NEW DELHI-110 002

Published by:
Tilak Wasan
DISCOVERY PUBLISHING HOUSE PVT. LTD.
4831/24, Ansari Road, Prahlad Street
Darya Ganj, New Delhi-110002 (India)
Phone: +91-11-23279245, 43764432
Fax: +91-11-23253475
E-mail: parul.wasan@gmail.com
info@discoverypublishinggroup.com
web: www.discoverypublishinggroup.com

First Edition: **2011**
ISBN: 978-81-8356-724-4

Printed at:
Shree Balaji Art Press
Delhi

Preface

Teaching profession is the noblest profession in the world. The profession got good respect in the society and the remunerations are good to lead a well family life. The status of teachers in present scenario is more upgraded. So prospective teachers are interested to join new colleges of education for duration of one academic year and they have to adjust in the new colleges with new fellow mates and new environment.

A good and proper adjustment in the college, with fellow mates and with the new environment leads to achieve good training and enable the prospective teachers for their enhancement of teaching skills. Adjustment is a harmonious relationship between the individual and the environment. It gives a balance situation in the mind.

The present study is intended to examine the adjustment of prospective teachers. It is thus, the degree of harmonious relationship that is maintained in striking a balance between ones requirements and the varying situations. The adjustment is embodied with many personality and environmental factors.

The book is very useful to the Teacher educators, Academicians, Psychologists, Teachers, Research scholars, University Departments of IASE, Education, and Psychology.

Dr. T.J. Mouni Suvarna Raju

Contents

Preface

1. **Introduction** 1

History of the word 'Adjustment'—Meaning of 'Adjustment'—The Process of Adjustment—Adjustment as Relatedness—Adjustment in Social Aspect—Definitions of Adjustment—Healthy Personality as Adjustment—Environmental Adjustment—Characteristics of a Well Adjusted Person—Need of the Study.

2. **Review of Research** 18

Adjustment and Gender—Adjustment and age—Adjustment and Marital Status—Adjustment and Branch—Adjustment and Medium—Adjustment and Social Status—Adjustment and Native Areas—Adjustment and Present Stay—Adjustment and Economic Status—Adjustment and Social Factors—Adjustment and Emotional Factors—Adjustment and Academic Factors—Adjustment and Health Factors—Adjustment and Environmental Factors—Adjustment and Training Programmes—Adjustment and Culture—Adjustment and Foreign Culture—Adjustment and Family Relationships—Adjustment and Parental Attachment—Adjustment and Parental Conflicts—Adjustment and Attendance—Adjustment and Personality Factors—Adjustment and Psychopathology—Adjustment and Drinking Behaviour—Adjustment and Other Studies.

3. **Methodology of Research** 66

Objectives of the Study—Hypotheses—Research Tools Used—The Adjustment Inventory—Indian

Adaptation of Bell's Adjustment Inventory—Variables Measured—Individual Variables—Sex—Age—Marital Status—Educational Qualifications—Branch—Medium—Social Status—Native Area—District—Present Stay—Parental Education—Teaching Parents—Parental Professions—Monthly Family Income—Type of Family—Adjustment Variables—Home Adjustment—Social Adjustment—Emotional Adjustment—Academic Adjustment—Health Adjustment—Total Adjustment—Data Collection—Administration of the Questionnaires—Language of the Questionnaire—Sample—Scoring of the Tests—Scoring of the Adjustment Inventory—Scoring of Indian Adaptation of Bell's Adjustment Inventory—Analysis of Data.

4. Results **92**

Adjustment Dimensions—Comparison across Sex—Comparison across Age—Comparison across Marital Status—Comparison across Educational Qualifications—Comparison across Branch—Comparison across Medium—Comparison across Social Status—Comparison across Native Area—Comparison across District—Comparison across Present Stay—Comparison across Parental Education—Comparison across Teaching Parents—Comparison across Parental Professions—Comparison across Monthly Family Income—Comparison across Type of Family—Interaction Effects—Interaction of Age and Gender—Interaction of Marital Status and Gender—Interaction of Educational Qualifications and Gender—Interaction of Branch and Gender—Interaction of Medium and Gender—Interaction of Social Status and Gender—Interaction of Native Area and Gender—Interaction of District and Gender—Interaction of Present Stay and Gender—Interaction of Parental Education and Gender—Interaction of Teaching Parents and Gender—Interaction of Parental Professions and

Gender—Interaction of Monthly Family Income and Gender—Interaction of Type of Family and Gender—Corelational Analyses—Inter Corelation Matrix of Adjustment Dimensions—Summery of the Results.

5. Discussion **124**

Adjustment Dimensions—Comparison across Sex—Comparison across Age—Comparison across Marital Status—Comparison across Educational Qualifications—Comparison across Branch—Comparison across Medium—Comparison across Social Status—Comparison across Native Area—Comparison across District—Comparison across Present Stay—Comparison across Parental Education—Comparison across Teaching Parents—Comparison across Parental Professions—Comparison across Monthly Family Income—Comparison across Type of Family—Interaction Effects—Age and Gender—Marital Status and Gender—Educational Qualifications and Gender—Branch and Gender—Medium and Gender—Social Status and Gender—Native Area and Gender—District and Gender—Present Stay and Gender—Parental Educational and Gender—Teaching Parents and Gender—Parental Professions and Gender—Monthly Family Income and Gender—Type of Family and Gender—Corelation Analysis—Inter Corelation Matrix of Adjustment—Summary.

6. Summary and Conclusions **139**

Findings of the Study—Conclusions of the Study—Recommendations of the Study—Suggestions for Further Research.

Bibliography 148

Index 165

History of the word 'Adjustment'

The word "adjustment" came in to popular use in psychology during the 1930's and was given strong endorsement by Lawrence Shaffer's classical book "The Psychology of adjustment" which was published in 1936. In his treatment of adjustment, Shaffer emphasized the biological adaptation of the organism to its environment as the central meaning of the term (Bell, 1962).

The term adjustment is often used as a synonym for accommodation and adaptation. Strictly speaking, the term denotes the result of equilibrium, which may be affected by either of these processes (Monroe, 1990). It is to emphasize the individual's struggle to get along or survive in his or her social and physical environment.

The concept of adjustment is as old as human race on earth. Adaptability to environmental hazards goes on increasing as the human beings proceed on the phylogenetic scale from the lower extreme to the higher extreme of life. Insects and germs, in comparison to human beings, cannot withstand the hazards of changing conditions in the environment.

Man, among the living beings, has the highest capacity to adapt to new situations. Man as a social animal not only adapts to physical demands but also adjusts to social pressures.

Biologists used the term adaptation strictly for physical demands of the environment but psychologists used the term adjustment for varying conditions of social or inter-personal relations in the society. Thus, adjustment means reaction to the demands and pressures of social environment imposed upon the individual. The demand may be external or internal to which the individual has to react. Chauhan (1979) and Vonhaller (1970) explained adjustment as 'psychological survival' in much the same way as the biologist used the term adaptation to describe 'physiological survival'.

"Life presents a continuous chain of struggle for existence and survival" says Darwin. The observation was apt since every one strives for the satisfaction of their needs. In struggling to achieve something, if one finds that results are not satisfactory, one either changes one's goal or procedure. While doing so one protects one's self from possible injury to one's ego, failure or frustration. It was shifted to more defensive position in order to face the challenge of circumstances after the initial failure. This special feature of the living organism is termed as adjustment in the view of Mangal (1989).

Every student from the beginning of his or her first grade until he or she finishes college education makes a long series of adjustments between the whole unique personality and the environment. The ardent desire of each boy or girl is to become an individual person having a healthy physique, a growing intellectual ability, a greater degree of emotional poise, an increased participation in social groups and such other characteristics that enhance personality.

Occasionally in the use of the term 'adjustment', the implication that the most desirable state of adjustment is one in which the individual is perfectly happy and satisfied with all aspects of life and one in which he had reached the level in all contacts with environment, that would be glad to persist throughout life. The best integrated and adjusted individuals would have established some reasonable goals in line with their interests, abilities and settled down to work towards those goals seriously and steadily, without unusual tensions. This implicated that adjustment means harmony between the individual and the environment.

Meaning of 'Adjustment'

The dictionary meaning of the word 'adjustment'is to fit, make suitable, adapt, arrange, modify, harmonize or make correspondent. Thus, when we make an adjustment between two things, we adapt or modify one or both of them to correspond to each other. In some situations, one of the factors may not be changeable and so the one which has to be modified in some way to suit the other. The extension of a ladder of a suitable length to reach an upper story window is a good example of such an adjustment. Wearing of clothes according to the requirements of the seasons is another such examples; ordinarily it is beyond our capacity, to change the seasons according to our clothes. Modern technology has made it possible to adjust the temperature inside dwelling houses and work places to harmonize with our needs.

The Process of Adjustment

Renuka and Anuradha (2004) described the process of adjustment in the following terms.

(1) Integration: A well adjusted student is able to concentrate his energies on his goal.

(2) Ego development: A well adjusted student is able to plan for the successful accomplishment of his goals.

(3) Reality orientation: A well adjusted student recognizes reality learners' frustration tolerance.

(4) Responsibility: A well adjusted student feels responsible and his certain freedom of emotional expression and self control.

(5) Sense of Security: A well adjusted student has a sound sense of security, which grows out of his feelings of belonging and being desired.

(6) Curiosity of Spontaneity: A well adjusted shows normal curiosity and exhibits a natural, easy,

spontaneity in a social relationship. Here adjustment means reaction to the demand and pressure of social environment imposed on the individual. The adjustment problem of the individual plays a decisive role in historical development. Such problems often have their roots at home and school.

Human adjustment is a never ending process (Ruch, 1970). It starts right from the birth of the child and continues till his death. It does not stop at any time rather it goes on with life.

The adjustment process is a universal sequence that can be identified in the behaviour of an organism from the lowest species up to man. Boring (1948) says that if a paramecium (single cell animal) meets an obstruction while swimming, it will backup, turn through a small angle and swim forward again.

Ray (1992) states that the question of adjustment arise, when there are certain demands or requirements that must be met or when one is confronted with problems and conflicts in various fields of life. Those must be resolved in some way or other. One creates a world of interpersonal relations and satisfactions that contribute to the continuous growth of personality. Human behaviour takes its character from the personality, which it expresses.

Odera (1995) concluded that the psychological stress might be created in an individual during the process of learning how to cope with a novel situation. The learning of new responses, skills and acquisition of new information help in coping with a new environment. However, the adaptation to unfamiliar situation should be taken as a special case of responding to an alien environment.

Kulshrestha (1979) explained that adjustment is the out come of individual efforts to deal with stress and meets his needs and the adjustment process is away in which the individual attempts to deal with stress, tensions, conflicts etc., and meet his needs. In this process the individual also makes efforts to maintain harmonious relationships with the environment.

Adjustment is a process by which a living organism maintains balance between its needs and the circumstances, which influence the satisfaction of these needs. It is therefore, a state of harmony between the needs, activities, resources of a person and the condition of his milieu (Boring, 1948). An individual not only adapts biologically to different kinds of physical demands and pressures, but also needs to adjust psychologically and emotionally, as he has to live and lead the life in interdependence with other individuals through out his life.

Lazarus (1976) states that adjustment consists of the psychological processes by means of which the individual manages to cope with various demands or pressures. Thus, adjustment is concerned with values. One cannot think of adjustment without being sensitive to the good and the bad or to the right and the wrong. Adjustment is that which brings to a person and to his social group the good and protects him from the bad.

Adjustment as Relatedness

Adjustment is a personal matter. Every individual makes a unique adjustment and every individual has unique ways of adjusting. No two people have exactly the same experiences in life, nor do they have exactly the same capacities for meeting their experiences. Getzels (1975) states, that no two individuals are alike even when they are presumably performing the same role. Each individual stamps the role with the characteristic style of his own personality.

An individual has been adjusted simply because he is alive. The outer forces acted on him, required him to change and deal with whatever capacities were available to him. These forces originate in his biological needs, other people and his cultural milieu.

Life is a continuous interplay of such forces many of which are created by the individuals and many of which are not, but regardless of their sources they demand responses from the environment (Coe, 1972).

Adjustment in Social Aspect

In adjustment the two crucial factors were the individual and the environment. In the study of the individual, the considerations were the heredity and biological factors, the psychological factors and the quality of socialization given to him where as, the environment includes all the social factors.

Adler's (1930) view that social interest may be regarded as one of the important determinants of adjustment because the individual has to adjust in a social situation.

How far one is adjusted can be ascertained by one's social development and adaptability to the social environment. Social adjustment requires the development of social qualities and virtues in an individual. It also requires that one should be social enough to live in harmony with his social beings and feel responsibility and obligations towards his fellow beings, society and country (Prasad, 1993).

A significant aspect of psychological adjustment is adjustment with other people. In popular usage, it is likely to regard a person as a well-adjusted person who 'gets along' with other people. Such a person may be pleasant, considerate, likable and socially deft.

In simple words, adjustment is an all-inclusive term meaning relationship between an individual and his environment through which his needs are satisfied in accordance with social demands. A person is said to adjust, when he is so related to reasonably adequate environment that he is relatively happy, efficient and has a certain degree of social feeling.

Dandekar (1981) states, that a well-adjusted person accepts his limitations. He does not blame others for his deficiencies. He does not run away from challenging situations. When he meets with a conflict he tries to resolve it on sound basis. Tallent (1978) says that, well-adjusted people are regarded as successful in the art of living.

Definitions of Adjustment

Many psychologists, sociologists, biologists and environmentalists defined adjustment. Some of the related definitions are presented in this section. Most of the definitions were given by the psychologists.

Warren (1934) defined as adjustment refers to any operation whereby an organism or organ becomes favorably related to the environment or to the entire situation, environmental and internal.

Good (1945) defined psychological adjustment as (i) Process of finding and adapting modes of behavior suitable to the environment or to change in the environment.(ii) Biologically as a change or acquired characteristics in an organism, that enables it to meet the requirements of its environment.

Webster (1951) defined adjustment is the establishment of a satisfactory relationship, as representing harmony, conformance, adaptation or the like.

Drever, James (1952) defined adjustment means the modification to compensate for or meet special conditions.

Shaffer (1952) defined adjustment as 'tension reduction'.

Shaffer and Shoben (1956) defined as "Life consists of a series of such sequences in which needs are aroused and satisfied. This family pattern is the process of adjustment".

Shaffer (1956) defined the relationship, which becomes established among the biological heritage of organism, the environment and the personality is adjustment.

Crow and Crow (1956) defined an individual's adjustment is adequate, wholesome or healthful to the extent that he has established harmonious relationship between himself and the conditions, situations and persons who comprise his physical and social environment.

Lindgren (1959) defined adjustment as the act or process of establishing a satisfactory psychological relationship between the individual and his environment.

Smith (1961) defined a good adjustment as one, which is both realistic and satisfying. At least in the long run, it reduces to a minimum the frustrations, the tensions and anxieties, which a person must endure.

Shaffer (1961) defined adjustment as the process by which a living organism maintains a balance between its needs and the circumstances that influence the satisfaction of these needs.

Bhatia (1965) defined adjustment as an all-inclusive term meaning relationship between an individual and his environment through which his needs are satisfied in accordance with social demands.

Gorlow (1968) defined adjustment as the co-ordination of the individual needs and goal seeking behavior into smoothly functioning interaction with the environment.

Bhatnagar (1968) says that adjustment refers to harmonious relationships between the individual and environment, where as social integration enhances efficiency, co-ordination, co-operation and communication

Coleman (1969) defined adjustment as the outcome of the individual's efforts to deal with stress and meet his needs.

Vonhaller (1970) defined we can think of adjustment as psychological survival in much the same way as the biologist used the term adaptation to describe physiological survival.

Gates and Jersild (1973) defined adjustment as a continual process by which a person varies his behaviour to produce a more harmonious relationship between himself and his environment.

Eysenck (1975) defined adjustment as a state in which

the needs of the individual on one hand and claims of society on the other hand are fully satisfied.

In a general way, personal adjustment is the process by which an individual applies his resources to fulfill his personal needs and maintaining harmony with the environment.

Different psychologists have defined adjustment differently but the investigator has taken the meaning of adjustment as "the degree of harmonious relationship being maintained in striking a balance between ones requirements and the varying situations."

Healthy Personality as Adjustment

A number of theorists have chosen to emphasize the function of personality in mediating the adjustment of the individual. Personality consists of the varied and yet typical efforts at adjustment that are carried out by the individual (Hall, 1978). One of the major contemporary views of personality is that it is molded by the individual's efforts to meet the demands of daily living. Thus, a personality is considered to be maladjusted when the individual is unable to adapt to the requirements of the social group of which he is a member. In short, the sum of the individual's movements as he adapts himself to the environment is personality. Instead of being a thing in itself, personality becomes a consensus of what can be observed about the actions of a human being.

Thorpe (1965) stated that psychologists who favour the adjustment view consider the data of personality to be valid only to the extent that they emerge from behaviour itself.

O'Connell (1974) states that the term personality, in seventy years ago was regarded as mental health. The concept of an average person can be treated if he adjusts to the society. In recent times also, some psychologists defined healthy personality as adjustment. According to Eysenck's (1978) personality is more or less stable and enduring organization of a person's character, temperament, intellect and physique, which determines his unique adjustment to his environment.

Allport (1961) defined personality as the dynamic organization within the individual of those psychophysical systems that determine his unique adjustment to the environment.

Human beings constantly strive toward goals, which gratify their biological and psychological needs. Sometimes people reach their goals with relative ease but when their needs are frustrated i.e. unsatisfied needs it, causes maladjustment in the person. The unsatisfied physical needs are generated by deficits in the organic structure and chemical balance of the body, the psychological and social needs are both natural drives and urges are learned. Both types of needs create tension in the individual, which leads to action (goal seeking). When an individual is blocked in reaching a goal, he may seek to reach the goal with renewed vigour, adopt a substitute goal (signs of a realistic and well adjusted person), try to reach the original goal by devious means (signs of being an unrealistic and offensive person) or withdraw into a world of fantasy (indicating maladjustment).

Human adjustment is thus, a never ending process of dealing with frustration. The adjusted personality is the normal representation of needs while the exaggerations lead to maladjustment. The adjusted personality is one, which bears a realistic relation to physical and social facts. In simple words, well-adjusted people tend to have a reasonably accurate evaluation of themselves in relation to their world and hence have a fairly realistic level of aspiration. Maladjusted people on the otherhand, tend to be unrealistic to set their aspirations either too high or too low leading to inevitable failure (Sharma, 1972).

Environmental Adjustment

This refers to the degree of harmonious relationship being maintained in striking a balance between one's requirements and the varying situations in a college. The prospective teachers spend most of the time in the colleges of education. At the time of data collection, they will visit to communities, in various societies. During the internship and intensive training they will practice in attached high schools. So the environments related to a prospective teacher are college environment, social environment, school environment and home environment.

Takahashi and Majima (1994) investigated the framework of social relationships that affect adjustment to the transition from home to the college campus dormitory. They concluded that the same age dominant type students easily developed the social relationships with new age mates. This study indicates that the individual factor like age, affects the social adjustment in hostel students.

In another study Barthelemy and Fine (1995), attempted to identify residence hall factors that enhance adjustment to college. They concluded that, for both men and women personal support and group cohesiveness were positively correlated with most adjustment dimensions. Also for women, group cohesiveness was positively related to academic adjustment and personal-emotional adjustment. For men, personal support and order were positively correlated with academic adjustment.

Thus, the studies clarified that the better adjustment leads to better academic achievement, better personal-emotional adjustment and better group relations.

The term 'college of education' refers to the place of study and training for prospective teachers studying 'Bachelor of Education' course. The terms like 'teacher training', 'teachers training course', 'teacher education', 'secondary school education', 'secondary teacher education' etc., are popularly used terms for B.Ed course. The student obtains education in college of education can be treated as 'student teacher' , 'trainee teacher', 'trainee graduate', 'prospective teacher' etc. The researcher selected the term 'prospective teacher' because it is quite suitable and more meaningful.

Characteristics of a Well Adjusted Person

Mangal (1989) states that a well-adjusted person is supposed to possess the following characteristics:

(1) Awareness of his own strengths and limitations:-A well adjusted person knows his own strengths and weaknesses. He tries to make capital out of his assets in some areas by accepting his limitations in others.

(2) Respecting himself and others:-The dislike for one-self is a typical symptom of maladjustment. An adjusted individual has respect for himself as well as for others.

(3) An adequate level of aspiration:-His level of aspiration is neither too low nor too high in terms of his own strengths and abilities. He does not try to reach for the stars and also does not repent over selecting an easier course for his advancement.

(4) Satisfaction of basic needs:-His basic organic, emotional and social needs are fully satisfied or in the process of being satisfied. He does not suffer from emotional cravings and social isolation. He feels reasonably secure and maintains his self esteem.

(5) Absence of a critical or fault-finding attitude:-He appreciates the goodness in objects, persons or activities. He does not try to look for weaknesses and faults. His observation is scientific rather than critical or punitive. He likes people, admires their good qualities and wins their affection.

(6) Flexibility in behavior:-He is not rigid in his attitude or way of life. He can easily accommodate or adapt himself to changed circumstances by making necessary changes in his behaviour.

(7) The capacity to deal with adverse circumstances:-He is not easily overwhelmed by adverse circumstances and has the will and the courage to resist and fight odds. He has an inherent drive to master his environment rather than to passively accept it.

(8) A realistic perception of the world:-He holds a realistic vision and is not given to flights of fantasy. He always plans, thinks and acts pragmatically.

(9) A feeling of ease with his surroundings:-A well-adjusted individual feels satisfied with his surroundings. He fits in well in his home, family, neighbourhood and other social surroundings. He likes his college, college-mates, teachers and feels satisfied with his daily routine. When he enters a profession, he has a love for it and maintains his zeal and enthusiasm despite of all odds.

(10) A balanced philosophy of life:-A well-adjusted person has a philosophy which gives direction to his life while keeping in view the demands of changed situations and circumstances. The philosophy is concerned around the demands of his society, culture and his own self so that he does not clash with his environment or with himself.

Need of the Study

Several studies have been reported in the areas of social, educational, health and emotional adjustment of campus prospective teachers of both sexes. Some studies try to relate adjustment with variables like intelligence, achievement, age, sex, socio-economic status, needs, anxiety and security. Prospective teachers' reaction to frustration has also been studied. A few studies focused on the nature, causes and extent of indiscipline among prospective teachers. The relation between indiscipline and variables like achievement, participation in co-curricular activities etc., were also examined.

Although University Departments of Psychology and Education have undertaken quite a few studies in the area of adjustment, much still remains to be done (Mitra, 1972).

In our Indian continent, more than 80% of people are dwelling in rural areas. The remaining people are living in urban and metropolitan areas. The situation is also same in Andhra Pradesh.

Like wise, the situation in North Coastal Andhra is also same. The North Coastal Andhra consists of three districts namely Srikakulam, Vizianagaram and Visakhapatnam. Among these three districts only Visakhapatnam city is just like the metropolitan type, but the other parts of the Visakhapatnam district are backward consisting of agency areas like Araku Valley, Paderu, Borra caves and Anantanag, Chintapalli forest zones. Vizianagaram district is very backward district among these three. There are very remote areas and even many mandals are undeveloped till now. Srikakulam district consists of two rivers namely, Nagavali and Vamsadhara. So, it has better agricultural development and the district is developing day by day in all aspects.

The students of these three areas are obtaining education from Andhra University and its affiliated colleges. The Andhra University headquarters are located at Visakhapatnam which has two campuses i.e. in Vizianagaram and Srikakulam towns of North Coastal Andhra. This year Srikakulam campus was become an independent university named as 'Dr. B.R. Ambedkar University'.

The student community obtains education up to their graduation in their native colleges. After completion of graduation, many students seek admission into B.Ed or Secondary Teacher Training Course. Students have to join the course by fulfilling the norms and conditions stipulated by the Ed-CET, APSCHE, NCTE and Andhra University, Visakhapatnam.

Teaching profession is the noblest profession in the world. So this profession got good respect in the society and the remunerations are good to lead a well family life. The three districts in question have an image and status for teachers. So prospective teachers are interested to join new colleges of education for duration of one academic year and they have to adjust in the new colleges with new fellow mates and new environment.

A good and proper adjustment in the college, with fellow mates and with the new environment leads to achieve good training and enable the prospective teacher for their enhancement of teaching skills. Adjustment is a harmonious relationship between the individual and the environment. It gives a balance situation in the mind.

Krishnan (1992) stated that the students who have completed their higher secondary or graduate education either in their own native places or in very nearby towns are constrained to move towards cities, where they have to face new environmental situations. Also, the students of all academic and professional courses constitute a group of heterogeneity and complexity, which is due to the variations prevalent among them in terms of region, locality, custom, language, style, caste, religion etc. It is in this context, the establishment of harmonious relationship with peer-groups assumes importance. The peer-group relationship is highly dependent on the adjustment of these students in their residence.

A review of the studies carried out in the field of adjustment as reported in the three surveys of Educational research edited by Buch (1991) reveals that no systematic attempt has yet been made to develop a tool for the assessment of adjustment of professional course entrants.

Bridges (1991) mentioned in psychological reports that the direct adjustment studies are reducing in West, with a similar title and with other psychological factors, the studies are in progress. Where as in India, the adjustment studies are very limited and a lot of work on adjustment is to be done. Concerned to students' adjustment, the works are more in western context and those works are limited in India. There is a necessity to conduct more studies on students' adjustment and environmental adjustments.

The researcher felt that there is a need to conduct a study on prospective teachers based on their adjustment with personality and environmental factors. The researcher selected some suitable individual variables to study on adjustments on prospective teachers to know the comparison of different independent variables across the different dependent factors.

More specifically, the research aims to examine the comparative adjustments of the prospective teachers based on their sex, age, marital status, educational qualifications, branch, medium, social status, native area, district, present stay, parental education, teaching parents, parental professions, monthly family income and type of family.

Gender acts as an important independent variable in prospective teachers adjustments. Girl prospective teachers adjustments are differ from the boys. In the same way prospective teachers of 25 years and above shows one type adjustment and certainly it would differ with that of the prospective teachers below 25 years of age. Age acts as an important demographic variable in the prospective teachers' community.

Marriage gives a peaceful atmosphere when it is successful. So the researcher wants to know the adjustments of married and un-married prospective teachers. The researcher wants to know whether the higher qualification may be shown any difference in the adjustment or not. So the variable 'educational qualifications' was incorporated in the present study.

Basing on the specializations of prospective teachers the 'branch' variable is selected. It would be possible to understand the differences of adjustments in various faculty back grounds. The researcher wants to know the adjustments of prospective teachers from both English and Telugu medium back grounds. So, the variable 'medium' was incorporated in the present study.

The researcher wants to know the adjustments of different community prospective teachers. So the variable 'social status' is incorporated in the study. The variable 'native area' was incorporated in the present study. The variable native area gives the justification about the variation of adjustments of the prospective teachers based on their native place. It is also called as locality or place of residence in other researches.

The North Coastal Andhra consists of three districts namely Srikakulam, Vizianagaram and Visakhapatnam. So the variable 'district' was also incorporated in the study to know the adjustments of the three district prospective teachers. The researcher incorporated the variable 'present stay' to compare the difference in adjustments of prospective teachers based on their stay in the duration of the course.

The researcher wants to know whether the parental education influence adjustments in prospective teachers or not. So the variable 'parental education' was incorporated in the study. Here the researcher wants to know whether the children of a teacher is in the teacher course or not, and the adjustment levels and their difference of such prospective teachers. Secondly how far the influence of father or mother took place in their adjustment levels. So the variable 'teaching parents' was incorporated in the study.

The variable 'parental professions' was incorporated in the study because it exhibits various adjustments of prospective teachers based on their parents' working back grounds. Another important variable that is, monthly family income played a vital role as it is interlinked with all other variables.

Here the researcher wants to know the adjustments of the prospective teachers came from nuclear and joint families. So the variable 'type of family' was introduced in the study.

The study is useful to know more about the comparison between groups in various dimensions of adjustment and also to know more about the relationships of various dimensions related to adjustments.

After identifying the problem for the study, the researcher gathered the information and material from various sources related to college environments, prospective teachers' adjustments, personality factors with adjustments and the relative studies, comparative studies on adjustments. All these related studies are reviewed in the next chapter.

CHAPTER 2 Review of Literature

The present study examines the adjustment of prospective teachers. The term 'adjustment' was an older concept, which enhanced the number of studies. The studies exploring relationship between adjustments and influenced by various demographic factors are incorporated in his section.

The cited studies are gathered based on the independent, individual and adjustment factors. The closely related studies like family relationships, parental attachments, parental conflicts, personality and self factors, environmental and situational factors, training programme and attendance, culture and foreign culture, psychopathology and drinking behaviour are adopted for the review studies. This chapter for convenience is categorized into different sections. The cited studies related to both Indian and foreign contexts are collectively framed in this chapter.

Adjustment and Gender

The studies conducted on male and female are mentioned in this section. Number of studies have done on the adjustment of sex, but clubbed with other dimensions are incorporated and reviewed in the following studies.

Rim (1989) examined about the self-confrontation and coping styles of 20 male and 20 female undergraduate students. Sex was found to be a moderating variable with males and females' results differed. Findings resemble those from a study indicating a relationship between extraversion and neuroticism, self-confrontation and coping styles.

Ponraj and Packiam (1993) conducted a study on adjustment problems of 50 adolescent students. The results revealed that girls were well adjusted in home, school, society and health in comparison with boys. Religion makes an impact on the adjustment of the adolescents in home, school, society and health. Caste is also influencing the adjustment of the adolescents.

Swami (1993) conducted a study on adjustment of 264 male/ 277 female orphan students in comparison with 264 male / 277 female normal students. The conclusions are normal students were better adjusted than orphan students. Normal male and normal female students were better adjusted than the corresponding orphan males and orphan females. Thus sex had no effect on the relationship of adjustment of orphan and normal students. The adjustment of orphan male students was higher than the orphan females. The adjustment of normal female and normal male students was similar.

Street and Kromrey (1994) examined the differences in adjustment issues for 171 male and 160 female adolescent students. They found female students were more likely than males to experience difficulties with self-esteem, depression and anxiety. Males were more likely to experience difficulties with substance abuse.

Lakshmi (1998) studied the adjustment of androgynous (male & female) persons in different areas such as home, health, social and emotional. The sample consists of 100 individuals of which 50 were androgynous and 50 were hyper masculine males and hyper feminine females drawn from different sections of society. Results revealed that the adjustment of androgynous persons was significantly better in all four areas than that of hyper masculine and hyper feminine females.

Bhaskar Rao and Harshitha (2004) conducted a study on the adjustment of secondary school students. The sample consists of 200 secondary students with 100 boys and 100 girls from residential and non-residential schools under government and private managements. The Indian adaptation of Bell's adjustment inventory of Lalita Sharma was used for data collection. The results revealed that the secondary school students were with low adjustment. The non-residential school students were more adjusted than the residential school students, though both were with low adjustment. There was no significant difference in the level of adjustment possessed by the private and government secondary school students, though both of them were with low adjustment. There was no significant difference in the level of adjustment possessed by boys and girls, though both were with low adjustment.

Thus the studies indicated that the male and female students have significant differences between various dimensions of adjustment.

Adjustment and Age

The study conducted on age mentioned in this section. In many studies, the variable 'age' was measured with other dimensions.

Takahashi and Majima (1994) investigated by using 26 weeks of longitudinal data on 61 Japanese female first year college students, this study examined how the pre established frame work of social relationships of an individual student affect adjustment to the transition from home to the college campus dormitory. In the results, as predicted the age mate dominant type students more easily developed relationships with new age mates and reported fewer difficulties in making the transition than their family dominant type counter parts.

Thus, the variable 'age' influences various types of student adjustment factors.

Adjustment and Marital Status:

The studies conducted on marital status and adjustments are included in this section.

Grant, Smith, Sinclar and Salts (1993) examined the impact of natural parent or custodial parent marital status on college adjustment and the impact of age at parental divorce on college adjustment. Sample consists of 341 freshmen, 65 of which were from divorced homes. Results indicated that marital status does not influence the adjustment of the students where as age at the time of parental divorce affected the student adjustment.

Carter, Elizabeth (2006) studied about the work of three fold 1) to examine the relationships between college student independence, parental support and assistance and college adjustment and achievement 2) To examine differences in these relationships based on parental marital status and income, gender and first generation student status 3) To provide policy recommendations for practitioners to assist them in making decisions about college student relationship with parents. The tools are 1) Parental support and assistance instrument and psychological separation inventory 2) Student adaptation to college questionnaire. Findings indicate that college student's emotional independence was positively related to college student adjustment for students from intact and high income families. Unexpectedly for students from non-intact and low income families functional, emotional and attitudinal independence form parents were negatively related to adjustment in college. For all groups parental support for autonomy was negatively related to college related activities was positively related to college student independence. Policy recommendations are suggested to help practitioners assess the positive and negative impact of parental assistance for college students.

The second study indicated that marital status influence on different types of adjustments.

Adjustment and Branch

The study adopted from the Indian literature conducted on branch and adjustment.

Rajan, Ashrafullah and Rajan (1988) studied about the adjustment problems of professional and non-professional students. The sample consists of 346 college students out of which 134 professional and 212 non-professional students. The important findings are the non-professional science students have a better level of adjustment than the professional students only in the emotional area but not in the social and educational areas. The professional students have a better level of adjustment than the non-professional arts students in the educational area but not in the emotional area. The non-professional arts students have better level of adjustment than the professional students in the social area. The non-professional science students have a better level of adjustment than the non-professional arts students in the emotional and educational areas but not in the social area.

The study indicated that the various differences among the different branches in student adjustment.

Adjustment and Medium

The studies conducted on language and adjustments are adopted for this section.

Kasinath (1991) conducted a study of adjustment between migrated Hindi and non-Hindi speaking students studying in Jawahar Navodaya Vidyalaya. The sample consists of 235 students among 52 urban/183 rural and 201 boys/ 34 girls and 197 non-Hindi speaking / 38 Hindi speaking students. Results indicated that there are some variations in Hindi speaking and non-Hindi speaking students in the areas of Social, Educational and Emotional adjustments.

Barrat and Huba (1994) studied about the factors related to international undergraduate student adjustment in an American community. 170 international undergraduates completed a mail survey assessing motivation, self-esteem, interpersonal relationships, participation in activities, English language skills and community adjustment. In the evaluation, students showed good adjustment in English language skills with self-esteem in interpersonal relationships.

Stuart Marcia Ciscely (2002) carried out a study among a group of English speaking under graduate students from the Caribbean, enrolled at a private, historically black university. Two hypotheses looked at the difference between those students who were classified as internal and those who were classified as external with regard to (a) their psychological adjustment and (b) their adjustment to college. 75 students participated in the study. The scales are 1) Rolter internal-external locus of control scale 2) student adaptation to college questionnaire. 3) Demographic questionnaire. Results of two-way ANOVA indicated no support for the hypotheses for which investigated differences between gender categories as well as between age categories on overall adjustment to college. The relationship between age and psychological adjustment was not found to be significant.

Thus medium of instruction as well as English language communication skills play an important role in students' adjustment.

Adjustment and Social Status

The Indian study conducted on social status and adjustment was taken for the review.

Bajpai (1999) investigated the effect of caste belongingness on adjustment of high school girls. The study conducted on 400 high school girl students of which comprised of 176 general caste, 61 Backward caste, 134 scheduled tribe and 29 scheduled caste of Madhya Pradesh Results shows that in the level of adjustment inventory that caste belongingness influence adjustment in different areas.

Thus the variable 'social status' particularly in the Indian context influence adjustment of students in different areas.

Adjustment and Native Areas

The adjustment studies on student population conducted on areas or permanent place of residential location were taken from Indian literature.

Kasinath (1990) studied the factors underlying adjustment in Navodâya Vidayalayas. The study conducted on 68 students of which 50 boys and 18 girls, but the data of 20 urban and 28 rural students were taken into consideration. The findings of this study indicates that there is no significant difference in the total adjustment scores of urban and rural, boys and girls studying in Navodaya Vidyalayas in respect of their emotional, social and educational adjustment.

Sujatha, Gaonkar, Khadi and Katarki (1993) conducted a study on factors influencing adjustment among urban and rural adolescents was carried out in Dharward block of Karnataka State. The sample consists of 300 students taken randomly out of 152 students from urban and 148 students from rural areas. The study revealed significant differences in the adjustment of male and female adolescent students of rural area. Early and late adolescents from both the urban as well as rural area did not differ significantly in their adjustment. Significant association was found between academic achievement and adjustment level among rural respondents.

Alexander and Packiam (1998) designed to find out the adjustment problems of male and female school going adolescents from two neighboring and culturally similar groups, 157 students from Vellore town and near by villages involved in the study. Findings revealed no significant difference in the proportion of maladjustment among the urban students. Urban adolescents have more problems than the rural students. Mother's education influences urban adolescent's adjustment.

Renuka and Anuradha (2004) studied the socio-demographic factors of the conduct disorder children and understand the adjustment level of these children at school, family, peers, teachers and in general. The sample consists of 170 students studying 5, 6, 7 classes of municipal schools at urban and rural areas of Tirupati, A.P. The scales used are 1) Child behaviour questionnaire, 2) Socio-demographic details schedule and 3) Pre-adolescent adjustment scale. The study reveals that no significant difference in adjustment among girls in both urban and rural areas. But, a significant difference was found among boys. Peer group influence is found more among urban boys. It can be concluded that social work skills will be more useful to improving the child's life.

The studies conducted on rural/urban areas and the adjustment factors on student populations were various conclusions in the above studies. Majority of studies indicates that there is a significant difference between adjustment and rural/urban areas.

Adjustment and Present Stay

The studies conducted on present stay of students are mentioned in this portion.

Floyd (1988) examined the family experience and college residential adjustment. The sample consists of 42 undergraduates in living learning group. They found the possibility that early parental attention and orientation toward social inclusion would mediate the relationship between family socio-economic status and college living group satisfaction. Data did not support a mediation effect.

Barthelemy and Fine (1995) attempted to identify residence hall factors that enhance adjustment to college. The sample consists of 121 college students living in residence halls. In the results for both men and women personal support and group cohesiveness were positively correlated with most adjustment dimensions. Conflict was negatively related to social adjustment for both sexes, and to all adjustment dimensions for women. Also for women, group cohesiveness was positively related to academic adjustment and personal-emotional adjustment. For men, personal support and order were positively correlated with academic adjustment.

Mukhopadhyay, De, Chattopadhyay and Biswas (1996) examined the impact of socially disadvantaged conditions on the psychological arousal system. A sample of 120 women, aged 18 to 22 years was equally divided into four groups; Institutionalized orphans, deaf and dumb subjects living in a hostel for the deaf (DDH), normal subjects residing in hostels (NH) and normal subjects residing at home (NRH). Results showed that the normal hostel mates are a little bit high in emotionality.

Bettencourt, Charlton, Eubanks and Kernahan (1999) investigated whether collective self-esteem development and residence hall membership predict adjustment to college in 142 first year students. Results show that academic adjustment at the end of first year in college was predicted by development in collective self-esteem. Development in collective self-esteem was associated with improvements in adjustment to college from first semester to the second semester. Results also show that residential group membership could have positive influences on adjustment. Implications of these findings are discussed in terms of their ramification for students academic adjustment, as well as for understanding the role of positively valued social identification with a context related group in enhancing overall positive adjustment in that context.

The above studies revealed that the present stay influences the adjustment of students.

Adjustment and Economic Status

This variable is an important one in the field of Indian Education. Most of the adjustment studies are interlinked with the socio-economic status of the students. Some studies are adopted from the Indian context.

Khan (1991) examined the relationship of adjustment to personality factors like anxiety, ego strength, approval-seeking motive and personal background factors like socio-economic status, father's occupation, structure of family etc., among college students. The sample consists of 500 students out of 250 males and 250 females. The findings are based on the high and low scores (poor and better adjusted group) of the male and female respondents separately. Various personality and familial background factors have been found to affect on individuals adjustment.

Mohan and Kaur (1991) studied the adjustment of university research scholars in relation to their values and socio-economic status. The sample consists of 200 students out of 90 male and 110 female students. The adjustment inventory consists of questions in four areas of adjustment-home, health, social and emotional. Values were measured in terms of theoretical, economic, aesthetic, social, political and religious. The socio-economic status scale consists of questions pertaining of education, occupation and income of father. In the findings, adjustment was found to have a positive correlation with economic values and a negative correlation with religious values. However, no significant correlation was found between adjustment and SES. Faculty differences were found to be significant for home adjustment, emotional adjustment, total adjustment, theoretical values, aesthetic values, political values and SES. Sex was found to a significant determiner of health adjustment, emotional adjustment, and total adjustment, theoretical, aesthetic, social, political and religious values and socio-economic status.

Miya and Krishna (1996) examine the impact of socio-economic deprivation on adjustment of urban male college freshman. The sample consists of 166 deprived and 106 non-deprived students. Findings reveal that the deprived group had more health related adjustment problems than the non-deprived group. Home, social and emotional dimensions of adjustment could not discriminate between the deprived and the non-deprived groups. Bi-serial correlation analyses reveal that socio-economic deprivation had a significant positive relationship with health and emotional dimensions of adjustment.

Mishra and Singh (1998) determine the personality adjustment of graduate students belonging to high and low socio economic status. A sample of 400 subjects, 200 male and female graduates of high SES, and 200 male and female graduates of low SES, completed the personality adjustment inventory. Results reveal significant difference between high SES and low SES graduates, in the case of both males and females, in all the areas of personality adjustment such as health, home, social, emotional and economic status.

Nabi Ahmed and Abdul Raheem (2003) studied the relationship of the criterion variable academic achievement, with the three predictive variables intelligence, SES and adjustment of adolescents. A sample of 180 students is administered culture fair Intelligence scale by Cattle, R.B., and Cattle, A.K.S. Urban Socio economic status by Gyanendra, P.S., and Adjustment Inventory by school students by Sinha, A.K.P., and Singh, R.P., by applying regression analysis. The study reveals that all the three predictive variables i.e., intelligence, SES and adjustment have contributed significantly to the criterion variable i.e., academic achievement. The magnitude of the potential relationship or shared common variance is found to be 60.4%.The separate contribution is found to be 48.5% of intelligence, 3.7% of SES and 8.3% of adjustment to the academic achievement for the adolescents.

The economic status showed the influence on personality and adjustment of the students from the conclusions of the above studies.

Adjustment and Social Factors

The studies related to all the social aspects like peers, family, group relations, social support etc are included in this portion.

Berndt, Miller and Park (1989) examined 169 adolescents' perceptions of friends and parents influence on aspects of their school adjustment. The students perceived parents as more influential than friends. There were no significant relationships, however, between the measures of perceived influence and of student's own adjustment. Students who were better adjusted to school did not consistently report either more or less influence of friends.

Rice, Cole and Lapsley (1990) examined the relation between adolescent-Separation-individuation, family cohesion and college adjustment on large college student sample. The model specified that family cohesion; positive separation feeling and independence from parents would predict college adjustment. The results indicated that the positive separation feelings factor was a better predictor of college adjustment than independence from parents or family cohesion.

Defour and Hirsch (1990) studied about a social network approach of the adaptation of 89 black graduate students. Findings indicate that the black graduate students who were well in their academic aspect showed better adjustment and also fewer dropouts from the department.

Jay and D'Augelli (1991) assessed patterns of social support and adjustment to University life and a comparison of 84 African-American and 81 white freshmen. African-American students reported significantly less support available than white students, but this difference disappeared when family income was used as a covariate. African-American and white students did not differ in adequacy of social support. Even with family income and prior academic performance co-varied. African-American students grade point averages were significantly lower than white students. No differences in well-being were found.

Schwitzer, McGovern and Robbins (1993) investigated the interaction effects between goal instability and social support on college adjustment. The study conducted on 113 college freshmen. Results declared that students with low goal instability who perceived a high level of support had higher levels of semester end adjustment than students who perceived a low level of support. The former used the available social support, both within and outside the classroom, to more effectively adjust to the university environment. Students with moderate levels of goal instability were not affected by social support.

Robbins, Lese and Herrick (1993) investigated the interaction between social support and goal instability to predict adjustment to college life for 198 freshmen students prior to this research, Schwitzer et al (1993) investigated the same topic in another university. In the results high-goal directed individuals showed better social adjustment.

Zakahi, Jordon and Christopher (1993) studied about the social adjustment to college: Communication apprehension and social network development among college students. The study concluded on 88 college students revealed that students with high communication apprehension (CA) adjusted more quickly to new social environment compared to low and moderate CA.

Reggio, Watring and Throckmorton (1993) examined the interrelations of the social skills inventory and various self-report measures related to the psychosocial adjustment of 136 undergraduate college students. Possession of social skills was positively correlated with perceived social support and most of the measures of psychosocial adjustment. Social skills combined with perceived social support predicted certain aspects of adjustment, particularly satisfaction with college. Students showed satisfaction with life in general, and reduced perceptions of loneliness.

Howie, Jessica Danielle (2004) study pointed out to determine the relationship between friendship group ethnicity and college adjustment for African-American students and the extent to which the students' ethnic identity and the ethnic composition of the college moderate this relationship. African-American freshmen and sophomores from two institutions (one predominantly white and one ethnically diverse) participated in the study by completing surveys. Results revealed that students at both schools who had a higher percentage of African-American friends were better adjusted emotionally. Students at the predominantly white institution exhibited better social adjustment than those at the diverse institution. Additionally other factors in the larger college context including perceived diversity and perceived racial conflict were found to have an impact on adjustment.

Kiefer, Sarah and Ryan, Allison (2008) investigated the proposal that social dominance goals are an important, but overlooked, aspect of social goals for young adolescents' academic adjustment. Self reports of social goals(dominance, intimacy and popularity goals)early in the school year was used to predict subsequent engagement (self reports and peer nominations of effort toward school work and disruptive behaviour) and achievement (i.e. grades)when students were in 6th grade (n=718) and again after the transition to middle school when students were in 7th grade (N=656;52% African and American and 48%White; 52%female and 48% male).In line with hypothesis, social dominance goals were associated with maladaptive forms of engagement and low achievement in 6th and 7th grades. For intimacy goals, relations were more limited, but when found; these goals were associated with adaptive forms of engagement in 6th and 7th grades. Popularity goals were not generally associated with engagement or achievement. The exception was 6th grade African American girls, for whom popularity goals were associated with maladaptive engagement, (i.e., low effort, high disruptive behaviour and low peer nominations for trying hard and getting good grades).

Ryan, Allison, and Shim, Serena (2008) conducted two studies, investigated the proposition that social achievement goals (different orientations toward social competence) are an important aspect of young adolescents' social motivation..Study-1(N=153,6th grade students) established that different orientations toward developing or demonstrating social competence can be seen in young adolescents' responses to open-ended questions about their social goals and social competence.Study-2(N=217,6thgrade students)evaluated a new survey measure of social achievement goals for young adolescents. Exploratory factor analyses indicated a 3-factor model (social development, demonstration-approach and demonstration-avoid goals).Different social achievement goals were associated with distinct patterns of subsequent self and teacher reported social adjustment (pro-social, aggressive and anxious solitary behaviours as well as social worry, best friend quality and perceived popularity).Effects for social achievement goals were independent of perceived social competence and gender.

Rosemary, Closson and Wilma, Henry (2008) conducted a study on White under graduate students matriculating at the HBCU express less overt evidence of social adjustment barriers than black students at predominantly white students. Although white students reported a sense of under representation, they reported no direct experiences of overt racism and reported good relationships and strong support from the HBCU faculty. Differences between the social adjustment experience of white undergraduate students and a similar study of white graduate students are discussed. Student affairs practitioners are challenged to consider racial-consciousness raising co-curricular and curricular educational programme that can assist white students in enriching their temporary minority experience. The eight student participants averaged 19 years of age and (with one exception)had attended the HBCU for at least one year. Data were gathered through focus groups, a racial identity scale and a faculty support scale.

Heather, J. Smith (2009) conducted a study on 212 first year under graduates completed an authority interaction checklist every time they had a (self-defined)meaningful interaction with university authorities during the first two weeks of their first semester. Students' degree of university identification before they began the term moderated the influence of campus authorities' treatment quality on academic engagement three months later. These longitudinal data provide support for the argument that people who identify with the group the authority represents will interpret the authorities' behaviour as indicative of their value to the group.

The above studies revealed that the better social relationships lead to better adjustment.

Adjustment and Emotional Factors

The studies conducted on students emotional factors incorporated in this section.

Lapsley, Rice and Shadid (1989) examined the relationship between psychological separation and adjustment to college in 130 freshmen and 123 upper classmen. Freshmen tended to show more psychological dependencies on mother and father, and poorer social and personal-emotional adjustment to college than did upperclassman. A pervasive relationship was found between separation and adjustment. Sex effects also emerged, with women showing more psychological dependencies than men.

Gerdes and Mallickrodt (1994) studied on emotional, social and academic adjustment of 208 undergraduate college students. It was a longitudinal study of retention in the six years of duration. Results indicate that two different sets of items best discriminated among good standing students and among poor standing students. Generally emotional and social adjustment items predicted attrition as well or better than academic adjustment items.

Clinton and Anderson (1999) studied about the social and emotional loneliness: gender differences and relationships with self- monitoring and perceived control. The sample consists of 50 men and 50 women. The population was African-American people. Both men and women experienced emotional loneliness with variation in the causes.

The studies pointed out that the emotional factors influence various dimensions of students' adjustment.

Adjustment and Academic Factors

The studies done on students academic aspects were inserted in this section.

Smith and Baker (1987) studied about 61 first year college freshmen decidedness regarding academic major and adjustment to college. They concluded that a relationship between decidedness regarding academic major and college adjustment emerged during the second semester. Adjustment problems associated with lack of academic major are discussed.

Chartrand (1990) studied about a causal analysis to predict the personal and academic adjustment of non-traditional students. The subjects in this study were 179 non-traditional undergraduate and adult special students. The results indicated that the data were consistent with the major hypotheses advanced in the model. Self-evaluation and commitment to the student role both had a direct effect on student role congruence, which in turn had a direct effect on academic performance and personal distress.

Leong, Bonz and Zachar (1997) studied about the coping styles as predictors of college adjustment among 161 freshmen. Results show that academic adjustment and personal / emotional adjustment were related to the coping strategies, while social adjustment and attachment / goal commitment were not.

Lindgren, Beth Maxine (2003) examined to assess academic experiences, out of class room experiences and overall adjustment to college life of freshmen over the 1st year of the college at mid-western institutions and to compare them with students at 5 peer universities. Results indicate that Midwestern students in all race categories showed greater success adjusting to academic demands of college. Peer institutions enrolled more students in learning cluster / learning community courses and 1st year adjustment courses than the mid western institution.

Hinkle,Sara (2005) studied about helping 1st year students to adjust to college life has long been considered important to academic performance and overall satisfaction with college. However, much of their literature focuses on student retention as a measure of student and institutional success, while paying less attention to variations in adjustment among students who remain in college. This study used qualitative methods to discover and describe the experiences of a group of 12-1st year students participating in an academic pre-college programme and to discern how the programme influenced their adjustment to college. The study yielded a rich, thick understanding of students' pre-college, academic and social adjustment experience.

Robert W. Lent et al (2008) conducted a study on 252 students at a university in northern Portugal. They completed the measures of academic self efficacy, environmental support, goal progress and adjustment along with global measures of the positive effect and life satisfaction. Path analyses indicated that the modal fit the data well overall. As expected self efficacy and environmental support were predictive of goal progress and academic adjustment and the later was predictive of students life global satisfaction. Self-efficacy and positive affect were found to be reciprocally related to one another. Contrary to expectations, goal progress did not contribute uniquely to the prediction of academic adjustment or life satisfaction.

Margaret L. Kern and Howard S. Fried Man (2009) study gathered follow up data from the Terman life cycle study(N=1023)to examine how age at first reading and age at school entry relate to grade school academic performance, lifelong educational attainment, midlife health and mental adjustment and longevity across eight decades. Early reading was associated with early academic success, but less lifelong educational attainment and worst midlife adjustment. Early school entry was associated with less educational attainment, worse midlife adjustment and most importantly, increased mortality risk, personality, midlife adjustment and educational attainment partially mediated the school entry longevity association (controlling for age, sex, personal characteristics and home environment factors).

The studies indicate that the academic adjustment depends on many other psychological factors. The Indian studies conducted on student adjustment with relation to academic aspects were included below.

Sharma, Verma and Kumar (1989) studied about the relationship of achievement motivation, adjustment and self-concept with academic performance of the students at +2 stage. The sample consists of 155 students from Delhi. The results of the study revealed that out of three, two variables namely achievement motivation and adjustment had positive and significant relationship with academic performance. However, the self-concept of students was not found to be a facilitative or detrimental factor of academic achievement.

Ray (1992) studied the personality characteristics and adjustment variables related to academic achievement. The study conducted on 165 female college girls belonging to the families of high and low socio-economic status. The results concluded that home and health areas of adjustment influence academic achievement of female college students. Moreover, dominance, practical mindedness, self-sufficiency, control over emotion, intelligence, and the need for achievement are the important consideration for successful scholastic achievement. Hence, adjustment that involves maturity in human behaviour influences academic achievement.

Sood (1992) examined the academic achievement in relation to adjustment. The sample consists of 120 pre-engineering students of Ambala. Higher Secondary/ Pre-university final marks were taken as achievement. It is found that there is no significant relationship between achievement and adjustment.

Tiwari and Pooranchand (1994) conducted a study of adjustment among high and low achieving adolescents. 100 students out of 50 high achievers and 50 low achievers participated in this study. The findings concluded that high and low achieving adolescents significantly differ in home, social and emotional areas of adjustment. However, they do not differ significantly in health and school adjustment.

The above studies indicated that the academic adjustment influence various other dimensions in student adjustment.

Adjustment and Health Factors

The studies conducted on health aspect along with other variables were kept in this section.

Leong and Mallinckrodt and Kralj (1990) investigated the cross-cultural variations in stress and adjustment among 75 Asian and 129 Caucasian graduate Students. Asian students reported experiencing fewer stressful life events, fewer chronic health problems and fewer total physical health problems than did Caucasian students. There were no significant differences between the two groups, in terms of psychological health, but Asian students showed greater difficulties with memory and hallucination in relation to Caucasian's greater difficulties with drug use problems.

Pennebaker Colder and Sharp (1990) conducted work on "Accelerating the coping process" on the basis of their previous work, freshmen should evidence improved health after writing about their thoughts and feeling associated with entering college. The self reports of homesickness and anxiety were taken from the 130 students. By year's end, experimental subjects were either superior or similar to control subjects in grade average and in positive moods, no effects emerged as a function of when people wrote, suggesting that the coping process can be accelerated.

Iwata (1994) conducted a study on 130 Japanese students out of which 46 male and 84 female students participated, to investigate the relationship between intolerance of waiting-stress and health, while another set of 125 students participated in a study to investigate the relationship between intolerance of waiting stress and personality. In the results, correlation coefficients between intolerance for waiting-stress and health and personality measures were low but significant. Higher intolerance for waiting-stress was linked with greater physical and psychological symptoms and with maladjusted personality.

Bernard, Hutchison, Lavin and Pennington (1996) examined in three experiments, the relationship among health related constructs of ego strength, hardiness, self-esteem, self- efficacy, optimism and maladjustment in 589 college students. The results stated that there was a relationship between health and personality factors in the way of adjustment. However, healthy personality leads to healthy adjustment.

Thus the studies indicate that Asian students suffer with health problems and poor health leads to maladjusted personality.

Adjustment and Environmental Factors

The studies conducted on situational or environmental factors adopted for the literature.

Mooney, Sherman and Lopresto (1991) examined an internal academic locus of control, a high level of self-esteem and a perception that the distance from home was just right were related to four dimensions of college adjustment namely personal, academic, social and attachment. The sample consists of 88 female freshmen. Regression analysis revealed that each predictor variable significantly increased the overall predictive accuracy of college adjustment. No associations were found between actual distance and the various dimensions of college adjustment.

Carlisle-Frank (1992) reviews literature on the psychological, sociological and environmental factors associated with relocation. It is argued that relocation is a complex personal, social and environmental transition that not only changes location of housing but also alters activities and domains. These changes associated with moving are enduring and affect almost every aspect of the individuals' life situation.

Terry (1994) conducted a longitudinal study of 243 students to examine the stable and situational influences on coping. After three sets of responses in a period of time, the results indicated that there was evidence that stable factors did influence coping behaviour.

Brooks and Dubois (1995) investigated the individual and environmental predictors of academic and psychological adjustment during the first year of college in 56 students. Results showed that although individual variable (American College testing score, problem solving skills, surgency / intellect, emotional stability) were related most strongly to adjustment, environmental variables (social support, daily hassles and distance from home) made significant incremental contribution to the prediction of grade point average, social adjustment and psychological symptoms.

Sia, Ah-Hiok (2000) examined the social networking process of international students in their off-campus adjustment to the new environment. Based on the integrative theoretical frame work of environmental-human development, social support, and social network models, the study focuses on how an international student forms their social network. The purpose of the descriptive study is to help understand the process of developing supportive networks in student transition to the new environment. This study also explored the factors facilitating on the barriers impeding the process of network building. The findings of the study substantiate a more theoretically grounded understanding of social networking and international student adjustment to the new environment.

Patricia, Gale Harrist (2006) studied about the students entering institutions of higher education are often apprehensive because adjusting to college culture can be difficult.1st year students especially under represented populations, face many difficulties that can seriously delay or halt collegiate career. Research on adjustment to college has typically emphasized three broad categories 1) academic 2) social and 3) personal-emotional. Tools used are 1) Learning and strategy inventory 2) college students' expectations questionnaire. MANOVA statistics were used. The results of this study provide the difference on 1st year students' academic, social and personal-emotional adjustment at public university. Recommendations were made regarding future research and studies.

The above studies showed that the situational factors influence the process of adjustment.

Adjustment and Training Programmes

The studies conducted on adjustment in relation with training programmes were placed in this section.

Schwitzer, McGovern and Robbins (1991) used the utilization focused evaluation model, to evaluate the out comes of an orientation seminar on early adjustment of 113 college entering freshmen. Findings support the use of a freshmen seminar as an intervention for promoting early academic and social adjustment to college life. The seminar seemed successful at increasing students' knowledge of the university providing available support services and promoting adjustment to the campus social environment.

Abe, Talbot and Geelhoed (1998) studied about the effects of a peer programme on International student adjustment. 60 newly admitted international graduate and undergraduate students, the majority of whom come from Asian Countries participated in an International peer programme (IPP).Of these students, 28 IPP participants campus resource use and student adaptation to college questionnaire (SACQ). Scores were compared to those of 32 international students who did not participate in the peer programme. Results suggest that the IPP participants showed significantly higher social adjustment scores than the non-participants. Additionally, students from Asian Countries had more difficulty in adjusting to campus life than international students from Non-Asian Countries.

Oravecz, Joseph (2002) investigated about the factors in wilderness orientation programme that influence student adjustment to college. Focus group consists of 30 total students. The researcher used a mixed methods approach, employing both qualitative and quantitative methods in this study. Wilderness orientation did impact individual students' college experience. When the participants were given the opportunity to voice what they perceived as factors of the wilderness orientation experience that had an impact on their adjustment to college.

Morgan, Valerie Ann (2005) investigated to determine the effects of an outdoor experimental team building programme on the college adjustment of the 1st Semester freshman in learning communities at a diverse urban university. A total of 123 students participated with 61 students in the experiential group and 62 students in the comparison group. Independent samples t-test of the SACQ (Student adaptation to college questionnaire) scores for attachment to the institution, social adjustment and overall adaptation to college. The analysis revealed no statistically significant differences.

The studies declared that the training programmes are helpful to the students for better adjustment to colleges.

Adjustment and Culture

The studies conducted on culture and adjustments were adopted in this section.

Duckworth, Linda wing (2002) study focused on leadership involvement and cross cultural adjustment experiences of two under graduate international students, in order to better understand how international students become involved at the leadership level, become adjusted to living in the U.S. and to determine any relationship between leadership involvement and adjustment. Research indicates a positive impact of student involvement on cognitive and affective college student's outcomes, indicating an even greater impact on student development as a result of leadership involvement. Results of adjustment survey also consistently indicate positive international student rankings of the factor "Social interactions with host nationals" with the interaction always limited to leisure and recreational activities. One of the main purposes of this study was to examine other ways that international student leaders might demonstrate involvement in order to expand the meaning of the social interaction factor and determine a possible relationship with adjustment.

Douglas, Alan Andrew, Lees (2005) investigated to understand the academic and cultural factors that affected the adjustment of Kuwaiti students sponsored by their home government, a part of a unique formal educational agreement with the university in an accelerated six-year combined Bachelor of Arts in Biology and Doctor of Dental surgery curriculum programme. Semi structured interviews were conducted for obtaining data. Findings indicate that cultural adjustment issues, proficiency in English as a second language and the context in which education took place, affected learning and academic achievement.

Gajdzik, Patrycia (2006) examined the cultural adjustment of international graduate students as compared to American graduate students and to examine the factors that contribute to self-efficacy beliefs in students from both groups. The research was conducted at a private midsized university in Texas. The sample was stratified based on age and gender and consisted of 100 international graduate students and 100 American graduate students. Results indicate that general self efficacy beliefs and students perceptions of their cultural adjustment were not related to one another.

The studies showed that the cultural issues influence different student adjustment factors.

Adjustment and Foreign Culture

The studies conducted on foreign culture and adjustments were mentioned in this section.

Furukawa and Shibayama (1993) Studied to construct and discriminate function to prediction adjustment in foreign culture. It was the study of 123 Japanese adolescent students studied abroad in home stay for one year. The results declared that the Japanese students could not adjust properly in foreign culture and also suffered emotional distress.

Tanaka, Takai, Kohyama and Fujihara (1994) studied about the adjustment patterns of international students in Japan. The sample of this study consists of 237 international students among 70.2% male population in 7 national universities of Japan. Factors analyzed with respect to demographic traits showed that the Asian students were less adjusted than those of Western and Latin American cultures. Those more proficient in the Japanese language did not prove to be better off. Scholarship recipients were better adjusted than those who rely on private sources for fund.

Kaczmarek, Matlock, Merta and Ames (1994) compared the student adaptation to the college for 29 international and 57 U.S. Students. International students significantly lower on the social, institutional attachment and goal commitment. However, international students experienced a more difficult college transition than US students. They have had a more difficult time, seek appropriate assistance, as those who rated they had received significant help from a faculty member reported a significant increase in psychological and somatic complaints.

Chiu (1995) explored the influence of anticipatory fear, both on natural processes of adjustment for 39 Asian Foreign students during their first academic year in the US, and on the effectiveness of a cross-cultural orientation programme based on I.L. Janis (1985) stress inoculation treatment (SIT). Students with different levels of anticipatory fear differed in their responses to SIT, with the low-fear group showed the clear signs of benefit. Findings suggested that how a person responds to novelty and uncertainty was a key factor in cross-cultural adjustment.

Jou and Fukada (1995) examined the effect of source of social support on adjustment, used the measures of needed support, actual support and the disparity between the two, on 64 Chinese students in Japan. The possible sources of social support were Japanese professors, Japanese students, other foreign students and Japanese friends' off-campus. The results concluded that the students who have taken help or social support from professors adjusted better than those students who have taken social support from Japanese students.

The above authors (1996a) investigated adjustment of Chinese students in Japan and examined whether their adjustment differed according to their country of origin, gender, age, proficiency in the Japanese languages or length of residence. 89 Chinese and Taiwanese postgraduates in Japan completed rating scale measures of adjustment. Students from Taiwan scored higher on adjustment. Male students reported higher adjustment on academic and cultural social scales. Students with a longer period of stay or higher proficiency in the Japanese language had higher scores on adjustment.

The above same authors (1996b) examined the effects of personality and social support on adjustment of 33 Chinese Students in Japan. It was a longitudinal study and the responses were taken for 4 successive periods of just arrived, 3, 9 and 12 months. The results concluded that the social support was the positive predictor of adjustment.

Eassau and Trommsdorff (1996) examined whether 162 North American, 111 German and 92 Malaysian college students differed with respect to problem and emotion focused coping styles and studied the extent of variance within each cultural context and the relationship between physical symptoms and coping styles. Results showed that in dealing with academic problems, Malaysian students used more emotion, focused coping than other students. North American and German students with high scores and emotion focused coping experienced fewer symptoms; whereas the reverse relationship was found with the Malaysian group.

Furukawa (1997) conducted a study to examine whether or not the cultural distance influenced psychological adjustment of international exchange students. The study conducted on 211 Japanese students with a host of 23 countries around the world and before and after the 12-item general health questionnaire, Maudsley Personality Inventory and Cultural Distance Questionnaires were administered. The results indicated that greater the cultural distance more the psychological distress in the student community. Food played the greatest impact on the intercultural adjustment.

Campbell, Donald Bruce (2002) study looked closely at Caribbean students one of the international groups that make up a significant percentage of international students. The investigation focused on the students' point of view that gave them a voice and allowed them to share their experiences and views on issues around their college adjustment. Participating students' different levels of adjustment can be attributed to what activities and individuals they surrounded themselves with.

Ying, Yu-Wen and Han, Meekyun (2008) study examined variation in the prediction of adjustment in Taiwanese students by ethnic density. Total of 155 Taiwanese students were assessed via survey pre-departure and three times post-arrival in the United States. Hierarchical regression analysis showed students on campuses with fewer other Taiwanese peers, formed more friendships with Americans and developed greater English competence by the second semester than those on campuses with more Taiwanese students. Further more, homesickness, affiliation with Americans and English competence in the second semester predicted functional adjustment in the third semester among students at moderate ethnic density schools, while baseline English competence alone predicted adjustment in students on high ethnic density campuses.

Marie Vafors Fritz, Dorothy Chin and Valirie De Marinis (2008) conducted a study on the acculturation process generally contributes greatly to stress and anxiety levels among international students. Surveys were distributed to 246 students aged 17-51 at an ethnically diverse community in southern California, US. Analysis of variance was conducted to investigate group differences between students: permanent US residents' vs international students and permanent US residents' vs European and Asian students, respectively. No significant differences were found between international students and students with permanent US residency. However, when the international student population was sub-grouped by the above cultural regions a different pattern emerged. Difficulties of not being able to work and of socially related problems were perceived as more severe for the European Asian groups, while financial problems were hard for all three groups. The variable of language difficulties was harder for Asian students, while that of stress of being apart from family was harder for students from Europe. Findings are not only congruent with prior research results on international students but also demonstrate that international students with culturally diverse needs should not be considered as one homogenous group. It is suggested that educational systems need to properly adapt in order to accommodate international students unique cultural needs.

One study adopted from the literature, conducted on foreign students studying in Indian University.

Odera and Hasan (1995) studied about the problems of adjustment to a foreign culture. Out of 150 listed situations, 22 social situations were reported to encounter by 90% of 38 foreign students. The conclusions revealed that the problems faced by the foreign students are neither eliminated nor reduced. Counselling is necessary for foreign students; if the problem is acute then psychiatrist help is also needed for better adjustment. Thus the counseling programme of the Indian Universities should be improvised for the international students.

In most of the studies, Asian Students are less adjusted in Western Cultures. International students experienced more difficult college transition, as well as emotion-focused coping.

Adjustment and Family Relationships

The studies conducted on family relationships and adjustments were taken for review in this section.

Rao and Yadav (1992) studied the adjustment problems of 240 adolescent girls in relation to family size and birth order. The results revealed that as the family size increased, the degree of satisfactory adjustment decreased. The second born, in general, in all the families was found child more well adjusted. The increase of family size with an addition of lateral birth orders after the second born, had more negative effect on the first born, consequently the third and fourth born are better adjusted than the first born in the areas of home, health, social, emotional and in general adjustment.

Chaudhury and Basu (1998) examined the impact of parent-child relationship on the school achievement and adjustment of 105 adolescent boys. The results indicated that the pattern of mothering, significantly influenced school adjustment. Both mothering and fathering styles were associated with academic success, particularly, rejection and neglect from parents were found to be highly detrimental.

Wang, Jing (2003) examined to explore relationships among resistance characteristic and background factors determine relationships among resistance characteristic and adjustment problem areas, evaluate relationships among adjustment problem areas and background factors, and identify resilience characteristics and background factors which significantly predict adjustment. Two instruments were used for this study.1) The personal resilience questionnaire 2) Michigan international student problem inventory. The Sample consists of 289 students from two universities. Statistical analyses revealed that resilience characteristics were moderately correlated with background factors. Negatively correlated with adjustment problem areas and better correlated with adjustment problem areas than were background factors.

Natasha Datta (2003) study focused on family environment and academic performance in the initial adjustment period. Research questions explored the impact of 1) family support and 2) grade point average on adjustment at the end of summer programme and fall semester. A sample of 86 students participated in the study. Student adaptation college questionnaire was used. A statistically significant positive relationship between family support and adjustment to college was found during the summer programme and at the end of the fall semester.

Dewall, Deborah Ann Baker (2005) study explored the impact of family relationship dynamics on college student adjustment, measures for 61 first year first generation college students. Students volunteered to complete a self report questionnaire during their second semester of college, measuring psychological coping, family relationships and academic, social, personal- emotional and overall college adjustment. Family relationship interaction was not associated with academic or social adjustment outcomes. Psychological coping provided a significant main effect, after participating out prior achievement for student social, academic, personal-emotional and overall adjustment. Lower negative mood was associated with higher adjustment. Student prior achievement was also positively related to academic adjustment and overall adjustment.

Pettus, Karen Rosenbalm (2006) examined the relationship between parental monitoring and student adjustment and achievement of community college students. A sample of 322 students completed the student experiences in college survey to assess their perceptions of parental monitoring and their adjustment to college. The sample was representative of the college student body. Significant differences in parental monitoring, student adjustment and performance by gender and ethnicity were noted. Women reported higher levels of parental control, better academic adjustment and higher average Graduate Performance Aptitude than men. Men reported higher levels of social adjustments and satisfaction of college than women. Parental monitoring had significant direct effects on student adjustment and performance. Student disclosure had a direct effect on social adjustment and GPA while parental solicitation had a direct effect on social adjustment. Social adjustment served as a mediator between student disclosure and parental solicitation with college satisfaction and GPA.

The studies indicated that the family relationships influence the students' adjustment.

Adjustment and Parental Attachment

This section was included with parental attachment and adjustment studies done on college students.

Lapsley, Rice and FitzGerald (1990) assessed the relationship between late adolescent attachment to parents and peers and personal identity, social identity and adjustment to college, among 148 male and 105 female college students, 130 of whom were freshmen. In the results, freshmen scored higher on personal identity than did upperclassmen. Women reported less alienation from peers, had more trust and better communication with peers and had higher scores on personal identity and social identity.

Kenny and Donaldson (1992) studied about the relationship of parental attachment and psychological separation to the adjustment of 162 first year college women. Close and positive attachments were normative and adaptive to student's levels of functional and emotional separations were not related to adjustment. Most of the students believed that their values and attitudes were similar to their parents and attitude similarity was associated with adjustment, conflict independence or low levels of anxiety, guilt and resentment in the parental relationship was the dimension of separation-individuation most related to adjustment.

Schultheiss, Palladine and Blustein (1994) tested the hypothesis that the conjoint variance of psychological separation and parental attachment is more strongly related to college student development and adjustment. The study conducted on 73 female and 66 male college students. For college student development there was support for the conjoint hypothesis for the women but not for the men. For college student adjustment, there was no support for the conjoint hypothesis for the women and limited support for the men.

Rice and Whaley (1994) examined student parent attachment in 131 undergraduates. Students completed questionnaires about their quality of their attachment relationships and about their adaptation to college during the 3rd, 9th and 15th weeks of a semester. Attachment to both parents was consistently important for women's adjustment. For men, attachment to the father was an important predictor for adjustment only during the high distress period before the end of the semester.

Kenny and Rice (1995) reviewed the attachment model and its relevance for understanding the psychological mechanisms available for meeting the developmental and adjustment challenges of late adolescent college students. Attachment is then discussed on the concept of life-span development, stress, coping and adjustment. Existing research supports an escalation between secure parental attachment and adjustment for first year college students.

Strange (1998) studied about family context variable and the development of self-regulation in college students. This paper proposes the conceptual framework based on attachment theory. A sample of 465 students was surveyed with 104-item students' attitudes and perception survey. Positive adjustment to the college is the one of the dimension in this survey. Results show better adjustment for students living with their parents as well as for those living on their own.

Pfeil, lynn Rigle (2000) examined about the importance of the parental-adolescent relationship in college adjustment. According to attachment theory both positive connections to parents and support for autonomy are necessary for psychological growth and healthy functioning in adolescence and may help in the transition to college. Despite indications that African American have more difficulty in adjusting to college, they have been under represented in the literature of parental attachment and college adjustment. The purpose of the study was to examine the associations between parental attachments, attachment style and college adjustment in African American students. A divorce sample of 100 African American male and female undergraduate students at a large, predominantly white state university participated in the study. Participants completed parental attachment, attachment style, college adjustment and demographic questionnaire. This study contributes new information about the parental attachment, attachment style and college adjustment of African American students. This information can be used for those helping African American students' adjustment to college.

Thus the studies declared that the parental attachment plays a vital role in students' adjustment.

Adjustment and Parental Conflicts

The studies conducted on parental conflicts, parental divorce and adjustment were kept in this section.

Lopez (1991) examined about the patterns of family conflict and their relation to college students adjustment in 122 male and 332 female students. In the results, females and students who reported high levels of marital conflict in their current family environments evidenced lower personal college adjustment. Students' academic adjustment may be most at risk if they are conflictually dependent on both parents simultaneously, while their personal adjustment may be negatively affected by a conflictual relationship with one or both parents.

Nelson, Hughes, Handal and Katz (1993) examined whether the structural intactness of the family or perceived family conflict was related to young adult adjustment as assessed by measures of ego identity status and psychological distress. 285 undergraduates were classified as belonging to an intact 2-parent family or a non-intact family, and as coming from homes characterized by low, medium or high levels of conflict. Findings support the psychological-wholeness model, which posits family conflict as the critical variable affecting adjustment.

Hill, Celeste Harris (2005) focused on the prior studies of individuals experiencing parental divorce during childhood and adolescence indicate a pattern of post divorce mal adjustment on academic, social, psychological, emotional and behavioural measures. A lot of 684 college students from four universities in the south eastern region of the U.S. participated in the study. Although there were no statistically significant differences between the delayed divorce and intact family groups on measures of well-being and intimacy in inter personal relationships, mean difference were found on a measure of academic progress.

Alford, Linda (2007) examined the impact of parents inter parental conflict on the adjustment of African, American college students. Sample consists of 90 with Children's perception of inter parental conflict scale and college adjustment scale. The results showed that inter parental conflict regardless of family status significantly imparted adjustment in this sample of students. The study further found that gender, age at the time of neither divorce nor post divorce conflict impacted adjustment in this sample.

The studies showed that the parental conflicts influence various adjustment factors.

Adjustment and Attendance

The studies conducted on attendance and adjustments were kept in this section.

Martin and Dixon (1994) investigated the impact of orientation attendance and locus of control on the adjustment of 242 traditional full time college students to college life. Results indicated that students with an internal locus of control orientation scored higher on the freshman transition questionnaire, indicating more successful adjustment to college life. No relationship was found between attendance at freshman orientation and adjustment to college.

The above same authors (1989) studied the effects of freshman orientation and locus of control on adjustment to college on 315 freshman students. Results show that although locus of control seemed to have had an effect on students' adjustment to college, orientation attendance did not have any effect.

The results pointed out that there is no relationship between attendance and adjustment to college.

Adjustment and Personality Factors

The supported studies on personality and adjustment of student populations are included in this portion. The related studies purely based on self, self-confrontation, self-feelings, self-esteem etc., were abstracted in this portion.

Tobacyk and Driggers (1989) investigated the self-monitoring as a moderator of relationship between traditional religious belief and personality adjustment. Results of a test battery administered to 211 college students suggest that low self-monitors show the strongest adaptive effects of religious belief on personality adjustment.

Verma and Swain (1991) conducted a study to ascertain whether self-concept of adolescent students is a determining factor of their personality adjustment. The sample of the study comprised 200 subjects out of 100 males and 100 females. The present study attempted to investigate the differences in personality adjustment of adolescent students possessing high, average and low levels of self-concept. The findings of the study revealed that variations in self-concept produce differences in personality adjustment of adolescent students.

Singh (1992) investigated the student activism in relation to adjustment. The study was done on 200 students of post-graduate classes among 100 activists and 100 non-activists. The results revealed that the two groups of student activists and non-activists differed significantly in the area of different adjustments. The results further indicated that activists were generally poor in home, health, emotional, educational and overall adjustment while better in social adjustment in comparison to non-activist students.

Aspin Wall and Taylor (1992) drawing on cognitive adaptation theory, optimism, psychological control and self esteem were explored as longitudinal predictors of adjustment to college sample of 672 freshman. Controlling for initial positive and negative mood, the beneficial effects of optimism, control and self-esteem on adjustment were mediated by the non use of avoidance coping, greater use of active coping and greater seeking of social support. The results of a two-year follow-up indicated that self esteem and control predicted greater motivation and higher grades, controlling for college entrance examinations scores.

Ichiyama, Colbert, Laramore and Heim (1993) examined the relationship of self-concealment to psychosocial adjustment in 200 female and 144 male college students. They found that the self-concealment was significantly correlated with self-reported anxiety, depression, shyness and negative self-esteem. The tendency of self-conceal was also found to differently related to the adjustment variable as a function of sex.

Ramanaiah, Byravan and ThuHien (1996) construct validity of Weinberger's six-group typology of adjustment was investigated by testing the hypothesis that the six personality types have different personality profiles. 170 Psychology undergraduates among 84 men and 86 men students completed the Weinberger adjustment inventory and the revised NEO personality inventory. Results strongly supported the tested hypothesis.

Protinsky and Gilkey (1996) collected a random sample of 102 women students from a small private college were assessed concerning their levels of individuation, intimacy, intimidation, parental triangulation and personal authority. These concepts formed the construct of personal authority and were tested as to their relationship to self-esteem, physical health and college adjustment. Results generally supported better adjustment for those women who had higher levels of personal authority.

Graziano, Jensen-Campbell and Finch (1997) examined about the self can be conceptualized as a mediating agent that translates personality into situated good-directed activities and adaptation. This research used a level of analysis approach to link personality dimensions (Level-I) to self systems (Level-II) and the teacher ratings of adjustment in African American, Mexican American and European American students in the sample of 317 students. The results concluded that adjustment factor linked up with other personality factors like personality structure, personality development and age related adoptions to social context.

Greenier, Kernis, McNamara and Waschull (1999) examined the extent to which level and stability of self-esteem predicted the impact that everyday positive and negative events had on individual feelings about themselves .130 undergraduate participants recorded the most positive and most negative events that occurred each day Monday through Thursday for a period of two weeks. Students then indicated the extent to which they feel better or worse. The negative and positive events had a greater impact on personality factors. Self-esteem differed from one situation to other and in acceptance or rejection of social situations.

Balaisis, Mary (2004) examined the student adjustment at Vilnius University in Lithuania. Since breaking away from the Soviet Union, Lithuania has been a country undergoing profound transformation. This study examined the implications of the changes for student adjustment by assessing individualism and collectivism at the personality level, in terms of idiocentrism and allocentrism. There were 673 students who agreed to participate of more than 1000 invited. The results indicated that for perceived wellness, the mean for Vilnius University students fell very slightly above the normal range found for college student population in the United States. State and trait anxiety and depression fell within the normal range. Good adjustment was related to an internal locus of control, idiocentric self-orientation and perceived social support. An internal locus of control was the best predictor of adjustment.

The above studies indicated that many personality adjustment variables leads to student adjustment in a better way.

Adjustment and Psychopathology

The studies conducted on neuroticism, psychoticism and adjustment problems were placed in this section.

Chaudhary and Sinha (1992) examined the effect of extraversion and neuroticism on adjustment in four different areas of adjustment namely home, health, social and emotional adjustment of college students. Sample consists of 100 male students from Semi Urban Colleges. Results of high and low extraverts showed better social adjustment than low extraverts. High and low neurotic students differed substantially in all the four areas of adjustment.

Hussain and Kumari (1995) examined the relationship of H.J. Eysenck's (1963) personality dimensions of psychoticism, extraversion and neuroticism with ego strength and adjustment. 100 male college students participated in this study. Ego strength was negatively related to psychoticism and neuroticism and positively but non-significantly related to extraversion. Some areas of adjustment were related positively and others negatively acted with psychoticism, extraversion and neuroticism. There was a non-significant correlation between neuroticism and adjustment. High neuroticism or psychoticism was related to better adjustment. High ego-strength was related to lower psychoticism, neuroticism and greater extraversion.

Rehulkova, Blatny and Osecka (1995) studied about the adolescents coping styles: A relation to the temperament. The coping strategies are determined by extraversion and neuroticism .309 students were administered measures of coping strategy and personality. It was conducted that neuroticism was associated with coping strategies of the disengagement type, and extraversion with strategies of the engagement type.

Saklofske and Kelly (1995) examined the relationship between personality and coping strategies with 196 undergraduates among 146 women. Students completed the Eysenck personality questionnaire and the coping inventory for stressful situations. Neuroticism accounted for 37% of the variance in emotion-focused coping. Personality and gender were not substantial predictors of other coping strategies.

Halamandaris and Power (1997) investigated the relationship between the two broad personality dimensions of neuroticism and extraversion and dysfunctional attitudes, as well as the relationship between dysfunctional attitude, perceived social support, loneliness and general well-being during the transition to University life in 124 students. Results indicate dysfunctional attitudes correlate significantly with all the personality and psychosocial adjustment variables, and personality (Extraversion, Neuroticism, Self-esteem, Interpersonal trust) and dysfunctional attitudes contribute significantly to the prediction of perceived social support and psychosocial adjustment to university life.

Cherian and Cherian (1998) collected the information on the adjustment problems of first year university students in developed countries, but comparatively little is known about such problems in Asia and Africa. This study of a representative sample of 1257 first year students conducted at the University of the North showed that 33% of 85% of the first year students experienced various adjustment problems.

Debbie Chiodo et al (2009) examined the gender differences in prevalence and types of sexual harassment victimization experienced in grade 9 and how it contributes to relationship victimization and psychological adjustment 2.5 years later. A total of 1734 students from 23 schools completed self-report surveys on entry to grade 9 and end of grade 11.Self-reported data were collected on victimization experiences (sexual harassment, physical dating violence, peer violence and relational victimization) and adjustment (emotional distress, problem substance use, self harm, suicidal thoughts, mal-adaptive dieting, feeling unsafe at school and perpetration of violent delinquency). Separate analyses by sex were pre-specified. Sexual harassment victimization was common among boys (42.4%)and girls(44.1%) in grade 9, with girls reported more sexual jokes, comments and unwanted touch than among boys, and with boys reporting more homosexual slurs or receiving unwanted sexual content. For girls, sexual harassment victimization in grade 9 was associated with elevated risk of self harm, suicidal thoughts, maladaptive dieting, early dating, substance use, and feeling unsafe at school. A similar pattern of risk was found for boys with the exception of dieting and self harm behaviour. Sexual harassment at the beginning of high school is a strong predictor of future victimization by peers and dating partners for both girls and boys and warrants grater prevention and intervention efforts.

The studies declared that the psychopathology influences the students' adjustment.

Adjustment and Drinking Behaviour

The studies conducted on alcoholism and adjustments were incorporated in this section.

Garbarino and Strange (1993) examined the family systems of 118 college-age adult children of alcoholics and the consequences of that experience for the adjustment to college during the freshman year. Family environmental aspects and parental alcohol abuse were played an important role in adjustments.

Montgomery and Haemmerlie (1993) examined the relationship between adjustment to college, drinking patterns, and various aspects of student life e.g. Fraternity or sorority membership in 114 university students. While consumption of beer was not related to students' adaptation to college, consumption of hard liquor was related to both academic and personal-emotional adjustment. Also, belonging to a fraternity or sorority was negatively related to both academic and personal-emotional adjustment but was positively related to social adjustment and overall drinking behaviour.

Haemmerlie, Steen, and Benedicto (1994) investigated conflictual independence from parents, adjustment and alcohol use among 109 college students at a mid western technical university. Results showed that greater alcohol use was associated with having achieved less conflictual independence from parents, the most frequent and strongest relationships occurred with respect to the mother student relationship. The results suggested that the parent student relationship has an impact on late adolescent development and that it also may play a role in alcohol used by college students.

The studies explained that the drinking behaviour influences the students' adjustment.

Adjustment and Other Studies

The above mentioned studies related to the dimensions of personality and adjustment. There were so many other supported studies on personality and adjustment on student community. The closely related studies were mentioned in this portion.

Kenrick, McCreath, Govern and King (1990) examined the interaction of personality dimensions like adjustment, likeability, self-control, social inclination, intellections, dominance and taxonomy of every day settings. Interactions show some setting seen to allow more expression of some traits. Main effect shows some setting seen as more generally illuminative and some traits as more generally visible.

Rice (1992) aimed to (1) Chart late adolescent individuation from freshman to junior year in college (2) further examined previously reported sex differences in separation-individuation and college adjustment and (3) assess the within year and across-year association between individuation and adjustment. 130 students among 81 from junior year participated in this study. The results indicated significant increase in individuation from parents' overtime along most but not all dimensions of individuation for both men and women. Gender specific patterns of individuation/ adjustment emerged in freshman and junior year. In general, independence from parents in freshman year did not predict junior year college adjustment.

Chartrand (1992) studied by testing a model of non-traditional student adjustment, predictors and consequences of psychological adjustment were examined. Results supported the feasibility of the model. Academic and non-college environmental variables were predictive of institutional commitment and an absence of psychological distress, which in turn predicted intended continuance in school. Implications of the results were related to the special academic and personal needs of non-traditional students.

Holmbeck and Wandrei (1993) assessed the individual and relational predictors of adjustment in first-year college students. The sample consists of 286 students among 182 women and 104 men students. Findings revealed that the separation-individuation, family relations and personality variables were better predictors of adjustment than were the cognitive indicator or home-leaving status. Results also varied as a function of gender, less well adjusted men were more disconnected from significant others, where as less well-adjusted woman exhibited higher levels of separation anxiety and enmeshment seeking.

Lecci, Okun and Karoly (1994) examined life regrets and current goals, as predictors of psychological adjustment on 155 students. Relative to regrets, goals were perceived as more impact, important, controllable, achievable, socially supported and desirable and as occupying more time and energy. Further more, regrets contributed to the prediction of psychological adjustment after controlling for negative affectivity. A content analysis of respondents' regrets is presented and related to chronological age and gender.

Valentiner, Holahan and Moos (1994) investigated an integrative model of mediating and moderating mechanisms in the coping process was examined in a two year, prospective frame work with 175 college students using the single group and multigroup LISREL analysis. Results concluded that changes in adjustment had direct impact of the family support associated with psychological adjustment in coping process.

Tloczynski (1994) studied the opening up meditation, college adjustment and self-actualization. In their study, 45 subjects who were divided into groups for opining up meditation, relaxation and control using scores on the anxiety scales of the college adjustment scalars. High dropouts leaving 3, 4 and 3 subjects respectively in the meditation, relaxation and control groups compromised the data analysis.

Silverthorn and Gekoski (1995) assessed the relationship among stress from parental pressure, independence from parents, self-efficacy and adjustment to University in 963 first year undergraduates. Results showed there was a strong relationship between adjustment and social desirability along with personality factors.

Adan and Felner (1995) explored notions of ecological congruence and person environment fit by examining relationships among personal and family background characteristics and the adjustment of 188 freshmen entering either a traditionally and predominantly white college or a traditionally and predominantly black college. Results indicated that there was no relationship of inter-racial experience to white students. Black students attending predominantly white college prior to inter-racial experience was associated with better adjustment to college.

Damji, Clement and Noels (1996) examined the effect of situational variations of identity and their relationship to measure of psychosocial adjustment. Sample consists of 295 native Anglophone students. Results indicated that an exclusively Anglophone identity was related to a higher level depression, lower self-esteem and a higher level of stress than the other modes of acculturation, but only when the variability in identity with the English group was high, students who were committed to English identity experienced more psychological adjustment problems.

Weiss and Schwarz (1996) examined Baum rinds T3 conceptual frame work using a multiple informant design and an older adolescent population with 178 college students and their families as participants, the present study found many of the predicted relations between parent child - rearing style (Authoritative, Democratic, Non directive and Unengaged) and their adolescent children's behaviour in the 4 domains assessed: personality, adjustment, academic, achievement and substance use.

Henning, Ey and Shaw (1998) studied the psychological distress; perfectionism and imposter feelings were assessed in 477 medical, dental, nursing and pharmacy students. Consistent with previous reports, the results showed that a higher than expected percentage of students (27.5%) were currently experiencing psychiatric levels of distress. Strong associations were found between current psychological distress, perfectionism and impostor feelings within each programme and these character traits were stronger predictors of psychological adjustment than most of the demographic variable associated previously with distress in health professional students.

Fox, Daniel Paul (2000) studied about the first year experience course at UNC was conducted. Previous work examined such interventions in the context of retention almost exclusively. Although these studies produced positive results, interactive effects of significant variables have rarely been explored in the context of overall adjustment to college. The study intended to discover whether adaptation to college was affected by the experience. Subjects are 238 with 107 females and 131 males. Results indicated no significant difference between students who participated in the course and those who did not, or between males and females or for other minority students. The researcher concluded that adjustment to college was not enhanced by the experience of being in the course.

Vanita Singh and Neeru Jasuja (2001) investigated to explore the difference in adjustment, leisure time activities and scholastic achievement of cable TV viewers and non-viewers in Indian conditions. Finally 100 matched pairs were selected as a sample individually on age, sex and intelligence scores. The tools consists of 1) Self prepared questionnaire to differentiate between cable TV viewers and non-viewers.2) Ravens progressive matrices 3) Adjustment Inventory by Mittal 4) Leisure time record blank prepared by the investigator, to keep record of out of school activities of students. 5) Achievement scores from the school record of students. Results showed that significant difference in the adjustment particularly total adjustment of cable TV viewers and non-viewers. Significant differences were found in leisure time activities of cable TV viewers and non-viewers. Significant differences were found in scholastic achievement of cable TV viewers and non-viewers.

Hadley, Wanda (2002) research study explored how students with learning disabilities adjust to the new expectations of higher education as they transits from K-12. The study focuses on students with the learning disabilities of dyslexia or reading problems through checkering vectors of college student development. The study was conducted on the campus of a private, four-year selective, co-educational college in the Midwest in 2001. The study sample of 9 was a small number chosen from a total population of 26 students with dyslexia and reading problems. The data were gathered through individual students' artifacts, two different focus groups and semi-structured individual interviews.

Kelly, Warren (2006) examined whether multi racial young adults reported lower levels of well being relative to their white and mono racial minority peers and whether these out comes were moderated by college attendance and racial identification. Sample consists of 615 multiracial, 4,686 mono racial minority, 9,343 white students. Therefore the current study found evidence of fewer difficulties of multiracial young adults relative to their mono racial peers. Implications for practice and future research are discussed.

Reynolds Shaw, Kathleen (2006) investigated about the idea that 1st generation college students have a harder time adjusting to college than to 2nd generation college students with respect to academic, social, personal-emotional adjustment, goal commitment, institutional attachment and overall adjustment. Students' adaptation college questionnaire tool was used. Participants were 112 students drawn from a 4-year liberal arts college in western New York. The 1st four SACQ variables under examination resulted in no statistically significant differences between 1st and 2nd generation college students adjustment.

In review of literature on the two major areas of personality or self-factors and environment or situational factors have indicated the need to conduct further study in this area, in spite of consistent relationships being observed. The line of action suggested that adjustment of prospective teachers in various dimensions like personality and environmental factors. The present study makes a humble attempt in this direction. The methodology adopted to conduct the study is presented in the next chapter.

This chapter describes the methodology adopted in the present study. It involves various independent and dependent variables thsat influence the prospective teachers on their adjustments, the method used for data collection, the suitable tools for the measurement of variables and the appropriate statistical measures for testing the hypotheses.

Objectives of the Study

(1) To examine the adjustment of prospective teachers and the impact of individual factors on their adjustment.

(2) To examine the impact of gender interactions of individual variables on adjustments.

(3) To examine the relationships between adjustment dimensions.

Hypotheses

1. Individual variables will have a significant influence on adjustment.
2. The interactions of individual variables will have a significant influence on adjustment.
3. Adjustment variables are expected to have a significant relationship between them.

The methodology adopted to study these hypotheses is discussed in the following pages, under different sections.

Research Tools Used

Two standardized questionnaires were used for the present study. They are 1) The adjustment inventory, constructed by Srivastava and Govind Tiwari (1986) and 2) The Indian adaptation of Bell's adjustment inventory, constructed by Lalita Sharma (1988).

The Adjustment Inventory

The adjustment inventory has been developed by Srivastava and Govind Tiwari (1986) for use with graduate and postgraduate college students. The preliminary form of the inventory had 130 'yes-no' type of items on the following areas of home, educational, emotional and social adjustments. The items were constructed by careful study of the relevant literature and help was taken from the tests of Asthana's Adjustment Inventory, Mittal's Adjustment Inventory, Bengal's Youth Adjustment Analyzer, Saxena's Adjustment Inventory and Kumar's Revised Adjustment Inventory.

The preliminary forms were submitted to a group of five judges. Items which were not approved by the judges were discarded. In the pilot form 120 items were included. Bi-serial correlation method was adopted for item-analysis. Thus 90 items were retained which yielded bi-serial correlation of each item with the total scores and with the area total scores. To bring down the number to 80, ten more items were eliminated. In the final form there are only 80 items covering the above said four areas of adjustment.

The inventory has been prepared both in Hindi and English. Ordinarily an examinee takes about five to ten minutes in answering the test.

The reliability coefficients have been found by three methods. They were Spilt-half method (0.91), test-retest method (0.95) and Kudar-Richardson formula-20 (0.93). For test-retest reliability, the inventory was administered on a sample of 225 students and after two weeks time the inventory was re-administered. The correlation between two scores was calculated by Pearson's Product Movement method.

Only highly diagnostic items were included in the final form of the test. Moreover, item-analysis was done each item by bi-serial correlation method.

The validation criterion used for this test was to correlate the scores of this present inventory with the scores of other valid and standardized tests on adjustment. Adjustment inventory for college students constructed and standardized by Sinha and Singh on 200 subjects, correlations found to be 0.70., and Adjustment inventory constructed and standardized by Mittal,V.K., again on 150 students the correlation was found to be 0.73.

Indian Adaptation of Bell's Adjustment Inventory

The original Bell's Adjustment Inventory was in English and for the purpose of standardization in Indian conditions it was translated by Lalita Sharma (1988) in Hindi. The Hindi version of the Inventory was given to five experts for its translation into English. Then, both the versions of inventory was given to ten experts who know both Hindi and English well, and asked for rating on five point scales on accuracy for translation, understandability and semantic equivalence on the basis of experts rating, the standing tables were prepared for scores of each item and these items above low standing scores, they were again translated. The present inventory consists of 80 items, retained as a result of item-analysis out of 140 items.

High scores on the Inventory indicate the good adjustment; where as low scores indicate poor adjustment in different areas of adjustment as well as adjustment taken as a whole. The numbers of items related to each area of adjustment are given in the Manual. Two categories of responses 'Yes-No' have been provided for answer to each item.

For determining of Validity co-efficient of the present inventory, the English version as well as the Hindi version of the inventory was administered to 100 higher secondary school going pupils who know well both Hindi and English languages. The validity co-efficient was found to be very high 0.834.

The validity of the present Inventory again checked through the administration of original Bell's adjustment Inventory and the present English version to a sample of 100 pupils with an interval of one week. The co-efficient of correlation was 0.812 which show the present Inventory as a valid measure of adjustment in Indian conditions.

Variables Measured

The present study has examined two types of variables namely, the individual and adjustment variables. The individual variables are sex, age, marital status, educational qualifications, branch, medium, social status, native area, district, present stay, parental education, teaching parents, parental professions, monthly family income and type of family.

The adjustment variables are home adjustment, social adjustment, emotional adjustment, academic adjustment, health adjustment and total adjustments.

The details regarding these variables are provided in the following pages:

Individual variables

The individual variables included in the present study are sex, age, marital status, educational qualifications, branch, medium, social status, native area, district, present stay, parental education, teaching parents, parental professions, monthly family income and type of family.

Sex

It was categorized into male and female prospective teachers. In any research the variable gives the differences between male and female counter parts. In the present teacher education institutions, the strength of female prospective teachers was more when compared with males. The study of the sex variable gives the difference of adjustment in between male and female prospective teachers.

It was the common variable in so many researches. In order to study the problem in detail, it is very essential to differentiate sex. As a recent trend in education and to up lift the woman education, Indian government implemented the rule of reservation that 1/3rd of the total seats were reserved for woman. So girl students are getting two way admissions in women reservation and on merit basis. On that aspect the comparative ratio of female prospective teachers was more in colleges of education.

Street and Kromrey (1994) examined the differences in adjustment issues for male and female adolescents. They have concluded that, female students were more likely than males to experience difficulties with self-esteem, depression and anxiety. Males were more likely to experience difficulties with substance use. The study conducted by Lapsley, Rice and Shadid (1989) also concluded that sex differences are present, with women showing more psychological dependency than men.

Lopez (1991) examined that female students who reported high levels of marital conflict in their current family environments evidenced lower personal college adjustment. Rice (1992) examined previously reported sex differences in separation-individuation and college adjustment. They found that gender specific patterns of individuation adjustment emerged in freshman and junior years.

In Indian studies Lakshmi (1998) found the differences between androgynous and hyper masculine males and hyper feminine females. Mohan and Kaur (1991) differentiate the sex based on different adjustment factors.

The above mentioned studies indicate that the sex variable has significant differences on adjustment of students.

Age

The variable age plays a very important role in student life. The minimum age of writing Ed-CET is 19 years and there is no upper age limit. The variable age was categorized by below 25 years and above 25 years. Generally below 25 years students are young, active and dynamic. But above 25 years students are experienced in many sociological, academic and psychological aspects. So the researcher wants to know the difference of adjustment between these two groups.

The minimum age for Sciences, Arts and Commerce backgrounds to study B.Ed course is 19 years. The minimum age group of all students from different faculties for the present study is 19 years. Most of the prospective teachers' population was in between the age group of 20-30 years. Based on this aspect, it was categorized into two groups i.e. below 25 years and above25 years with a gap of five years between the majorities of student population.

Takahashi and Majima (1994) investigated by using 26 weeks of longitudinal data on 61 Japanese female first year college students, this study examined how they established frame work of social relationships of an individual student affect adjustment to the transition from home to the college campus dormitory. In the results, the age mate dominant type students more easily developed relationships with new agemates and reported fewer difficulties in making the transition than their family dominant type counter parts.

The study indicated that the agemate dominant females are better in social adjustment. The age factor up to certain extent influences the adjustment of hostel students.

Marital Status

The variable 'marital status' is categorized into married and un-married prospective teachers. Generally women prospective teachers in colleges of education are mostly married and some are also having children. Married prospective teachers have to perform two functions. They have to look after their husbands, children at home and attend the classes, complete the academic work in colleges of education. Un-married prospective teachers are having fewer burdens, at present they perform only the academic work. The psychological problems are more for the un-married prospective teachers. Marriage gives a peaceful atmosphere when it is successful other wise it is a burden.

Grant, Smith, Sinclar and Salts (1993) examined that marital status does not influence the adjustment of students. Carter, Elizabeth (2006) study indicated that the non-intact families' functional, emotional and attitudinal independence from parents were negatively related to adjustment in college. So the researcher wants to know the adjustments of married and un-married prospective teachers.

Educational Qualifications

The variable 'educational qualifications' is concerned to the higher education. It was categorized into graduate and post-graduate prospective teachers. The minimum requirement for B.Ed programme was graduation. Only certain courses like B.A, B.Sc, B.Com, BCA and BBM are eligible for B.Ed course but the other bachelor degrees like B.L, MBBS and BOL are not eligible. The students who completed their Post-graduation or Research degrees can also apply and study the B.Ed course because there is no age restriction. Every academic year, few students with post-graduate degrees will get admission into B.Ed course.

The researcher wants to know whether the higher qualification may be shown any difference in the adjustment or not. So the variable 'education' was incorporated in the present study.

Branch

The variable 'Branch' was included to know the adjustment of different faculty prospective teachers. The variable branch is categorized into Biological sciences, Physical sciences, Commerce and Arts faculties.

Science under-graduates are having more workload than commerce and arts under-graduates. Apart from theory papers, science under-graduates have to strive hard for the practical work. But in the B.Ed course the special projects, practical work and theory are same for everyone. So there is a possibility of increase in the anxiety levels especially for commerce and arts graduates. Hence the variable gives the complete and actual facts related to adjustment of prospective teachers.

In order to study the problem as a whole in the colleges of education, it was suggested to choose more or less equal number of students for the present study among these four major faculties. By this detailed study, it can be understood the adjustments of each group and the comparisons among the four groups.

Mohan and Kaur (1991) studied the adjustment of Research scholars in the faculty-wise comparison. The faculty differences were found to be significant for home adjustment, emotional adjustment and total adjustment. Similar study was done by Rajan, Ashrafullah and Rajan (1988) concluded that non-professional science students have a better level of adjustment than the professional students only in the emotional area but not in social and emotional areas. The professional students have better level of adjustment than the non-professional arts students in the educational area but not in the emotional area. The non-professional arts students have better level of adjustment than the professional students in the social area. The non-Professional science students have a better level of adjustment than the non-professional arts students in the emotional and educational areas but not in the social area. The above Indian studies indicated the variations in the different levels of adjustments. Hence this faculty variable is an important one for the present study.

Medium

The variable 'Medium' was categorized into English and Telugu media prospective teachers. According to the norms of NCTE, Bangalore, the teaching in education colleges is only in English and B.Ed programme is a UG professional course. Recently AP government is also planning to establish the English medium B.Ed colleges. But in the North Coastal Andhra situated colleges of education, the instruction will be in Telugu and the prospective teachers are showing interest to listen in Telugu only. Majority of students came from the background of Telugu to the colleges of education. But in the present curriculum the paper of communicative English was introduced as a common paper, to train the prospective teachers in basic English language skills. So it is a difficult paper to the prospective teachers who came from the total background of Telugu medium. This leads to increase the fear about some subjects. Kasinath (1991) study revealed that there are some variations in Hindi speaking and non-Hindi speaking students in the areas of social, emotional and educational adjustments. Barrat and Huba (1994) study concluded that students showed good adjustment in English language skills with self-esteem in interpersonal relationships.

Hence the researcher wants to know the adjustment of prospective teachers from both English and Telugu medium back grounds. So, this variable was incorporated in the present study.

Social Status

Social stratification is the categorization of the person based on the caste system. The variable is categorized into OC, BC, SC and ST prospective teachers. OC students belong to the upper castes, and they are not getting any sort of scholarships in their study. Backward castes consist of number of communities with scholarship facility from the government whose annual amount is below rupees one lakh.

In Srikakulam district the dominant community is 'Kalinga', which comes under BC community. This community is sub-categorized into 'Kinthala kalinga' and 'Burugapu kalinga'. In Vizianagaram and Visakhapatnam districts the major BC community is Koppula Velama. Here the Kapu community is considered as Thurpu kapu which is recognized as BC community. Scheduled Caste communities are having fee reimbursement and scholarship facility. The Integrated Tribal Development Authority (ITDA) project was established at 'Seethampeta', of Srikakulam district. Most of the region in Vizianagaram district covers under agency area. ITDA project was established in Parvathipuram division. The ITDA project related to Visakhapatnam district was established in 'Paderu' division. Some students belong to ST communities will join B.Ed course. Ponraj and Packiam (1993) identified in their study that caste is also influencing the adjustment of the adolescents. Bajpai (1999) investigated that at the level of adjustment inventory that caste belongingness influence adjustment in different areas.

The researcher wants to know the adjustment of different community prospective teachers. So this variable is incorporated in the study.

Native Area

The variable 'native area' was incorporated in the present study. It is also called as locality or place of residence in other researches. The variable native area is categorized into urban, rural and agency areas. The urban population are less compared with rural area and the agency populations are very less. Each area has a lot of variation in their living styles and culture. The urban students are familiar with computer and technological skills along with the communication skills. Where as, these skills are less in rural and agency students. So the prospective teachers of rural and agency areas are prone to face the difficult situations in the B.Ed course.

Most of the prospective teachers came from the rural areas to study secondary teacher education in the colleges of education. The local area for the students of Srikakulam, Vizianagaram and Visakhapatnam districts are AU region. The majority of coastal area includes more number of villages and mandals with few towns. Villages and mandals constitute rural area and towns and corporations constitute as urban area.

Kasinath (1990) study indicates that there is no significant difference in the total adjustment scores of urban and rural, boys and girls studying in Navodaya Vidyalayas in respect of their emotional, social and educational adjustment. Sujatha Gaonkar et al (1993) study revealed significant differences in the adjustment of male and female adolescent students of rural area. Early and late adolescents from both the urban as well as rural area did not differ significantly in their adjustment. Significant association found between academic achievement and adjustment level among rural respondents. Alexander and Packiam (1998) study revealed no significant difference in the proportion of maladjustment among the urban students. Urban adolescents have more problems than the rural students. Renuka and Anuradha (2004) study found that no significant difference in adjustment among girls in both urban and rural areas. But, a significant difference was found among boys. Peer group influence is found more among urban boys.

The above Indian studies indicate that there is an influence of area on adjustment. The place of residence i.e. rural or urban or agency was an important variable to study in detail and comparison among them. Hence the variable gives the justification about the variations of adjustment of the prospective teachers based on their native area.

District

District is a unit of area with certain boundaries geographically. The North Coastal Andhra consists of three districts namely Srikakulam, Vizianagaram and

Visakhapatnam. Among these three districts only Visakhapatnam city is just like the metropolitan type, but the other parts of the Visakhapatnam district are backward consisting of agency areas like Araku Valley, Paderu, Borra caves and Anantanag, Chintapalli forest zones. Vizianagaram district is very backward district among these three. There are very remote areas and even many mandals are undeveloped till now. Srikakulam district consists of two rivers namely, Nagavali and Vamsadhara. So, it has better agricultural development and the district is prospering day by day in all aspects.

Here the investigator concentrates on the place of establishment of college in the district but not the native district of the student. The three districts are nearby districts and there is a possibility of prospective teachers to study in nearby colleges established in other districts. The researcher wants to know the degree of adjustment among the colleges of education established in the three districts. So the variable 'district' was also incorporated in the study to know the adjustments of the three district prospective teachers.

Present Stay

The variable 'present stay' is categorized into home, room and hostel resident prospective teachers. The duration of the B.Ed course is one year. So the out station students have to adjust by taking rooms on hire basis. The native students may attend from their home and the SC; ST students may reside in their respective hostels. The student needs of home resident prospective teachers can be easily fulfilled but for room and hostel resident prospective teachers the needs may not be fulfilled. So the anxiety levels of room and hostel resident students may be higher. B.Ed training course has a creative programme and the student teacher has to prepare teaching aids.

Floyd (1989) found the possibility that early parental attention and orientation towards social inclusion would mediate the relationship between family socio economic status and college living group satisfaction. Data did not support the mediation effect. Mooney, Sherman and Lapresto (1991) examined that no associations were found between actual distance from home and the various dimensions of college adjustment. Barthelemy and Fine (1995) identified that the residence hall factors enhance adjustment to college. Mukhopadhyay, De, Chattopadhyay and Biswas (1996) study results showed that normal hostel mates are a little bit high in emotionally. Bettencourt, Charlton, Eubanks and Kernahnan (1999) identified that the residential group membership could have positive influence on adjustment. So the researcher incorporated the variable 'present stay' to compare the difference in adjustment of prospective teachers based on their stay.

Parental Education

This dimension was categorized into both parents are educated, one parent educated and both parents are un-educated. Parental education is having a lot of influence on the children's education. In the observation the children generally choose the profession of their parents. In present social system teaching profession is a noble profession. So every parent whether educated or un-educated wants to send their children to the teacher education course. Alexander and Packiam (1998) in their study found that mother's education influences urban adolescents' adjustment.

Here the researcher wants to know whether the parental education influence adjustment in prospective teachers or not. So the variable parental education was incorporated in the study.

Teaching Parents

The variable 'teaching parents' was categorized into both parents are teachers, only father teacher, only mother teacher and both parents are not teachers. The variable 'teaching parents' was incorporated in the study because there is a notion that many children choose their parental profession as their profession.

Here the researcher wants to know whether the children of a teacher are in the teaching course or not, and how far such prospective teachers are adjusting. Secondly how far the influence of father or mother took place in their adjustment levels. The variable incorporated in the study will show the difference of adjustment of prospective teachers either their parents working in teaching professions or other professions.

Parental Professions

The variable 'parental professions' was categorized into parents working in agriculture, parents working in private sectors, parents working in government professions and business parents of prospective teachers.

The variable was incorporated in the study to know the adjustment of prospective teachers based on their parents working backgrounds. Here the money earning as well as their status influenced the adjustment of prospective teachers. In the above mentioned professions private sector jobs are more critical with out job security. Agriculture and business are independent and individual professions. The government jobs have security with professional advancements and pension benefits after retirement. So the prospective teachers of the working parents in private sector have to face some adjustment problems. The variable may reveal the difference in the adjustment of prospective teachers based on their parental professions.

Monthly Family Income

The variable 'monthly family income' was also denoted as financial status or economic status in some other researches. It was the family monthly income from all sources. The income may depend on the jobs, business, agriculture or private professions. The income may not be fixed based on the profession. The variable was categorized into below Rs. 5,000, between Rs. 5,000 to Rs. 10,000, between Rs. 10,000 to Rs. 20,000 and Above Rs. 20,000.The 1st category may be considered as poor and the 4th category as rich groups and the 2nd and 3rd groups can be considered as middle class. Money doesn't play an important role in the life but it fulfills the needs and desires of a person.

Here the researcher incorporated the variable to know the adjustment of the prospective teachers based on their economic status. Generally poor parents face the financial problems and their children also influence the same.

Some Indian studies were done on the adjustment of students based on economic status and some studies were clubbed with social status along with economic status were done on the adjustment of students related to socio-economic status. Khan (1991) found that socio-economic status of the family has been significantly associated with adjustment of high and low female groups. Mohan and Kaur (1991) found the socio-economic status and adjustment of university of Research Scholars was related insignificantly. Miya and Krishna (1996) revealed that the socio-economic deprivation had a significant positive relationship with health and emotional dimensions of adjustment. Mishra and Singh (1998) found that personality adjustment was influenced by the socio-economic status of graduate students. Results reveal significant differences between high SES and low SES graduates, in the case of both males and females, in all the areas of personality adjustment such as health, home, social and emotional adjustments. Nabi Ahmed and Abdul Raheem (2003) study reveals that the variables intelligence, SES and adjustment have contributed significantly to academic achievement. The contribution is found to be 48.5% of intelligence, 3.7% of SES and 8.3% of adjustment to the academic achievement to the adolescents.

The above studies indicate that there is a relationship between socio-economic status and adjustment of students.

Hence this variable adopted for the present study to observe the relationship between adjustment and economic status of the prospective teachers.

Type of Family

The variable 'type of family' is categorized into nuclear and joint families of prospective teachers. In olden days the joint family systems were common and such type of families are mostly present in villages. But in urban setup, because of social situations nuclear families are formed. Most commonly parents and elders in the joint families help their sons and daughters. The elderly help was not there in nuclear family but parental help was there. Rao and Yadav (1992) study results revealed that as the family size increased, the degree of satisfactory adjustment decreased. Chaudhury and Basu (1998) study indicated that the pattern of mothering significantly influenced school adjustment. Both mothering and fathering styles were associated with academic success, particularly rejection and neglect from parents was found to be highly detrimental. Natasha Datta (2003) study examined that the statistically significant positive relationship between family support and adjustment to college was found during the summer programme and at the end of fall semester.

Here the researcher wants to know the adjustment of the prospective teachers came from nuclear and joint families. Sometimes the elderly pressures are more in joint families, which also lead to face some problems. The variable incorporated in the study shows the difference of adjustment of prospective teachers from the nuclear and joint families.

Adjustment Variables

The adjustment variables included in the present study are home adjustment, social adjustment, emotional adjustment, academic adjustment, health adjustment and total adjustments.

Home Adjustment

Home is the source of greatest satisfaction and security to its members. The relationship among the family members and their ways of behavior plays a leading role in the adjustment of a child. All problematic and delinquent behaviour is the result of that adjustment and mal-adjustment, to a great extent is the product of faulty bearing and uncongenial atmosphere at home. Ponraj and Packiam (1993) study indicated that religion makes an impact on the adjustment of the adolescents at home.

Home is a place for obtaining culture, knowledge, customs, traditions, religious things and so on. The measuring items related to elders of the family, brothers and sisters, parental love and affection, pleasant and happy home environment etc. This variable measures the degree of home adjustment of prospective teachers.

Social Adjustment

Social adjustment requires the development of social qualities and virtues in an individual. It also requires that one should be social enough to live in harmony with his social beings and feel responsibility and obligations towards his fellow beings, in college as well as in society. How far one is adjusted can be ascertained by ones social development and adaptability to the social environment. Social adjustment requires the development of social qualities and virtues in an individual. It also requires that one should be social enough to live in harmony with ones social beings and feel responsibility and obligation towards ones fellow beings, society and country.

The items related to the aged people, friends, working with others, talking with others, social programmes, joking, pleasure in meeting with others etc. The social adjustment dimension measures the degree of adjustment in social situations. It is an important dimension in the field of teacher education.

Schwitzer et al (1991) used the utilization focused evaluation model, to evaluate the outcomes of an orientation seminar on early adjustment of college entering freshmen. Findings support the use of a freshman seminar as an intervention for promoting early academic and social adjustment to college life. The seminar seemed to have successful at increasing students' knowledge of the university, providing available support services and promoting adjustment to the campus social environment. Same authors in 1993 declared that students with low goal instability who perceived a high level of support had higher levels of semester - end adjustment than students who perceived a low level of support. The former used the available social support, both with in and outside the classroom, to adjust more effectively to the university environment. Students with moderate levels of goal instability were not affected by social support. Robbins et al (1993) also support the above study. Zakahi et al. (1993) concluded that the moderate or high communication apprehension, adjust to a new social environment, more quickly.

In Indian studies Singh (1992) concluded that the student activists were generally poor in home, health, emotional, educational and overall adjustment while better in social adjustment. Tiwari and Pooranchand (1994) concluded that the high and low achieve significantly differ in social adjustment. Rajan, Arrafuallah and Rajan (1988) concluded that the professional and non-professional college students significantly differ in social adjustment. Mishra and Singh (1998) concluded that the low and high socio-economic students significantly differ in social adjustment.

The above studies showed the variable social adjustment influence on personality and adjustment of students. This variable measures the social relationships in college adopted for the present study.

Emotional Adjustment

Emotions play a leading role in ones adjustment to self and his environment. An individual is said to be emotionally adjusted if he is able to express his emotions in a proper way at an appropriate time. It requires ones balanced emotional development and proper training in the outlet of emotions. This variable is an important one and plays a leading role in one's adjustment to his environment. An individual is said to be emotionally adjusted if he is able to express his emotions in a proper way at a proper time. It requires ones balanced emotional development and proper training in expressing emotions. In extreme cases, a student must seek balance between the extremes of repression on the one hand and uncontrolled emotional expressiveness on the other; otherwise he becomes the victim rather than the master of this most potent force in his personality.

The items of this variable include the sadness, excitement, fear, angry, nervousness, jealous, anxiety, temperament etc. High emotionality found among students who are overtly nervous and excitable and those who present an unexpressive front to the world. Counseling alone however cannot do the entire job. The student must also find more effective action patterns than he has in the past through which to express his feelings. So the students of high emotionality are recommended for the counseling cell in psychology department of university campus.

Gerdes and Mallinckrodt (1994) studied emotional, social and academic adjustment of college students. It's a longitudinal study of retention in the six years of duration. Results indicate that two different sets of items best discriminated among good standing students among poor standing students. Generally emotional and social adjustment items predicted attrition as well or better than academic adjustment items.

In Indian studies Mohan and Kaur (1991) found the faculty differences in emotional adjustment and sex was found to be a significant determinant of emotional adjustment. Tiwari and Pooranchand (1994) concluded the significant difference in high and low achieving students in emotional adjustment. Rajan, Ashrafullah and Rajan (1988) studied the adjustment problems of professional and non-professional college students and found the differences in emotional adjustment. Mukhopadhya et al (1996) concluded that the normal hostelmates are a little bit high in emotionality.

All the above-mentioned studies indicate that the emotionality variable influence much in student adjustment. It is a reasonable and rational variable to measure in the present study.

Academic Adjustment

This dimension measures the degree of adjustment in academic aspects. Those students' wants to seek the high achievements in educational aspects needs better academic adjustment. The items related to the subject matter in class room, studies, cultural programmes, questioning, examinations etc. If the student suffers more of any of these aspects it creates maladjustment in academic aspect.

Smith and Baker (1987) concluded a relationship between academic and college adjustments and the adjustment problems associated with lack of academic major. Chartrand (1990) found that self-evaluation and commitment to the student role both had a direct effect on student role congruence, which in turn had a direct effect on academic performance and personal distress. Brooks and DuBois (1995) showed that although individual variables were related most strongly to adjustment, environmental variables made significant incremental contributions to prediction of academic and psychological adjustment.

In Indian studies Sharma, Verma and Kumar (1989) revealed that an achievement motivation and adjustment had positive and significant relationship with academic performance. Ray (1992) concluded that adjustment which involves maturity in human behaviour influence academic achievement. Sood (1992) found that there is no significant relationship between achievement and adjustment. Tiwari and Pooranchand (1994) concluded that high and low achieving adolescents significantly differ in home, social and emotional areas of adjustment.

The majority of above studies mentioned that the academic adjustment influence the personality adjustment of the students. Thus the academic adjustment variable measures the prospective teachers academic adjustment, has taken for the present study.

Health Adjustment

This dimension measures the degree of adjustment in health. A high score on health adjustment means that the student has reported that he has not had a history of physical illness and that the physical ailments he may have had, have not bothered him sufficiently to cause discomfort or that he has developed an accepting attitude towards them.

It should be emphasized that the health adjustment scores are dependent upon the accuracy of the students' knowledge of his own health history and on the amount of discomfort that his ailments may have caused him.

The items related to the cough and cold, fatigue, digestion, headache, tiredness, anxiety about health etc. The maladjustment creates in the college if the student suffers more with the problems. At that time, it was advised to consult the dispensary physicians of primary health centers.

Leong et al (1990) found that Asian students in foreign culture showed greater difficulties with memory and hallucinations. Iwata (1994) found that higher intolerance for waiting stress was linked with greater physical and psychological symptoms and with maladjustive personality. Bernard et al (1996) found the significant relationship between health and personality factors.

In Indian studies Mohan and Kaur (1991) in their investigation, sex was found to a significant determiner of health adjustment. Ray (1992) found that health adjustment influence academic achievement of female college students. Odera and Hasan (1995) studied about the problems of foreign students in Indian University. They suggested that the students who display deep emotional disturbances or the pathological systems require counseling at a deeper level and should be referred to counseling psychologist or a clinical psychologist or in some cases to a psychiatrist.

All the above mentioned studies indicate that the health adjustment dimension influence the personality adjustment. There is a popular saying that the 'Sound mind in a sound body' so that the good health adjustment leads to good personality adjustment. This variable reasonably selected to measure the health of the prospective teachers for the present study.

Total Adjustment

How far a prospective teacher is satisfied with his college environment related to infrastructure and institution facilities, its discipline, time-table, co-curricular activities, methods of teaching, class and classmates, lecturers and head of the institution is completely in the pattern of this total adjustment. Similarly, the occupational world of adults dominates their mode of adjustment. The Degree of satisfaction with the environment, learning conditions, relationship with colleagues and teachers, financial expenditure and the chances of improvement decide ones adjustment to college and contributors significantly towards ones overall adjustment. Mohan and Kaur (1991) study examined that faculty differences and sex differences were found for total adjustment.

The totality of home, social, emotional, academic and

health adjustment dimensions of adjustments make the total adjustment of a prospective teacher.

Data Collection

Data were collected from the Colleges of education affiliated to Andhra University, Visakhapatnam, from the three districts viz., Srikakulam, Vizianaaram and Visakhapatnam of North Coastal Andhra.

The data collected form the colleges of education in the months of June and July, 2008. The total colleges of education in Srikakulam district were 13 with the strength of 1380 students, in Vizianagaram were 18 with the strength of 1865 and in Visakhapatnam were 19 with the enrollment of 2100.The total strength of the prospective teachers at that time was 5345, from the total colleges of 50.

Administration of the Questionnaires

The researcher administered the questionnaires by group in each college of education. The subjects were asked to complete the questions in part-A, General information and in part-B, Individual information from the questionnaire. The researcher read the instructions loudly appearing on the beginning of questionnaire in part - A and part - B sections. After the subjects read out the instructions silently, the difficulties were asked and removed. Then the subjects were asked to begin marking the items. There is no time limit for marking the two parts, but normally 30-45 minutes time is required to complete the total questionnaire. In some instances, the researcher explains the questions in the questionnaire in certain cases of subjects feel ambiguous.

Language of the Questionnaire

The study held in Srikakulam, Vizianagaram and Visakhapatnam districts of Andhra Pradesh state, South India, and the mother tongue of this region is 'Telugu' language.

The students feel no difficulty in reading as well as understanding the questionnaire in English language. The questionnaire was also translated in regional language with the help of five language experts. The researcher clarified the doubts of the students whenever they feel ambiguous.

Sample

The researcher used the "Stratified random sampling" technique for sample collection. 21 colleges of education randomly selected 7 from each district for the data collection. The total questionnaires distributed were 1500 out of which 1400 filled questionnaires were considered as sample by eliminating the unfilled and partially filled questionnaires. The sample includes 506 male and 894 female students from selected group.

Among the sample, the strength of Biological sciences was 302 with 93 male and 209 female students. The strength of Physical science students was 542 out of 202 male and 340 female students. The strength of Commerce students was 84 with 27 male and 57 female students and the strength of Arts students was 472 with 184 male and 288 female students.

The prospective teachers from Srikakulam district were 510 with 181 male and 329 female students, from Vizianagaram district were 450 with 169 male and 281 female students and from Visakhapatnam district were 440 with 156 male and 284 female students. All together the size of the sample is (N=1400) which consists of 30% sample from the total population.

Scoring of the Tests

The scoring of the both adjustment inventory and the Indian adaptation of Bell's adjustment inventory are same.

Scoring of the Adjustment inventory

In the adjustment inventory, beside every item, 'yes/no'

responses are present. The inventory can be scored with the help of a key given in the manual. The scores can be obtained by counting the number of correct answers marked in each area of adjustment. The areas of adjustment are home, social, emotional and academic dimensions. The sum of scores in different areas provides measure of each adjustment. The high score indicates the better adjustment of prospective teacher.

Scoring of Indian Adaptation of Bell's Adjustment Inventory

In the Indian adaptation of Bell's adjustment inventory, beside every item, 'yes/no' responses are present. The inventory can be scored with the help of a key given in the Manual. The scores can be obtained by counting the number of correct answers marked in each area of adjustment. The areas of adjustment are home, health, social, emotional and total adjustments. The sum of scores in different areas provides measure of each adjustment .The high score indicates the better adjustment of the student teacher.

The responses of the prospective teachers to the questionnaires were assigned weightages in accordance with the variable being measured under the wording of specific items. The four adjustment dimensions home, social, emotional and academic adjustments were taken from the adjustment inventory and the health adjustment dimension was taken from the Indian adaptation of Bell's adjustment Inventory and the total of five areas of adjustment constitute the total adjustments of the subject. Both the Inventories are measuring the total six dimensions of adjustment.

Analysis of Data

The main objective of the present study was to examine the adjustment of prospective teachers. To achieve this objective the sample of 1400 prospective teachers have to be categorized into various factors like sex, age, marital status, educational qualifications, branch, medium, social status, native area, district, present stay, parental education, teaching parents, parental profession, monthly family income and type of family.

The data collected from prospective teachers were analyzed as follows:

1. t -tests were conducted to examine the significance of differences in mean scores of adjustments across the individual variables.
2. One-way analyses of variances (ANOVA) tests were conducted to examine the significance of differences in mean scores of adjustments across other independent variables.
3. Multivariate analyses of variances (MANOVA) tests were conducted to examine the significance of differences of interaction of gender and other variables on adjustments.
4. Pearson's product moment coefficients of correlation were conducted between the adjustment variables. These analyses would provide information regarding the relationships between the variables.

The next chapter followed by the complete information with regarding to the results.

The results of the study are presented in this chapter. The data have been analyzed to examine:

(1) The adjustament factors of prospective teachers and the impact of individual factors on their adjustment.

(2) The gender interactions of individual variables on adjustment variables.

(3) The relationship between adjustment variables.

The results are presented in three sections of the following pages.

Section I includes the results relating to the influence of individual variables on adjustment dimensions.

Section ll includes the results regarding the gender interactions of individual variables on adjustment variables.

Section III includes findings regarding the relationships between different dependent variables.

SECTION – I

ADJUSTMENT DIMENSIONS

The scores of each respective dimension of adjustment are computed and tabulated for obtaining the values of 't-scores and F-scores'. The mean scores measures the degree of adjustment in respective dimension. Higher mean scores indicate the degree of better adjustment in the respective dimensions. The significant 't-values and F- values' are mentioned more specifically in the results and the non-significant dimensions were neglected.

Comparison across Sex

The mean scores of adjustment dimensions across the male and female prospective teachers are presented in table-1. The comparison of the scores indicated that the two sex groups of prospective teachers differ statistically on home and emotional adjustment dimensions.

More specifically, it is observed that the differences are statistically significant across the home adjustment dimension ($t = 5.76$; $p < 0.01$) and emotional adjustment dimension ($t = 3.78$; $p < 0.01$).

Comparison across Age

The analysis of the data involved the comparison of the adjustment variables across the age groups i.e., Age below 25 years and Age 25 years and above. The mean scores and t-values are tabulated in table-2. It can be observed that the t-values obtained across the two age groups are not significant.

Comparison across Marital Status

The analysis of the data involved the comparison of the adjustment variables across the marital status i.e. married and un-married. The mean scores and t-value are tabulated in table-3. It can be observed that the t-values obtained across the two groups are not significant.

Comparison across Educational Qualifications

The mean scores of adjustment dimensions across the graduate and post-graduate prospective teachers are presented in table-4. The comparison of the scores indicated that the two graduate and post-graduate groups of prospective teachers differ statistically on home, social, academic and social adjustment dimensions.

More specifically, it is observed that the differences are statistically significant across the home adjustment dimension ($t = 3.15$; $p < 0.01$), social adjustment dimension ($t = 2.93$; $p < 0.01$), academic adjustment dimension ($t = 1.98$; $p < 0.05$) and total adjustment dimension ($t = 1.96$; $p < 0.05$).

Table 4.1. Gender and Adjustment
(N= 1400)

	Dimensions	Mean & S.D.	Males (N=506)	Females (N=894)	t Values
1.	Home Adjustment	Mean	15.24	16.22	5.76**
		S.D.	3.14	2.98	
2.	Social Adjustment	Mean	15.82	15.59	1.51
		S.D.	2.79	2.66	
3.	Emotional Adjustment	Mean	12.29	11.52	3.78**
		S.D.	3.77	3.59	
4.	Academic Adjustment	Mean	15.42	15.63	1.19
		S.D.	3.21	3.05	
5.	Health Adjustment	Mean	14.54	14.54	0.04
		S.D.	3.39	3.36	
6.	Total Adjustment	Mean	73.34	73.51	0.26
		S.D.	12.33	11.48	

**$P < 0.01$

Table 4.2. Age and Adjustment
(N= 1400)

	Dimensions	Mean & S.D.	>25 Yrs (N=993)	<25 Yrs (N=407)	t Values
1.	Home Adjustment	Mean	15.90	15.79	0.61
		S.D.	2.97	3.31	
2.	Social Adjustment	Mean	15.75	15.48	1.64
		S.D.	2.73	2.65	
3.	Emotional Adjustment	Mean	11.71	12.01	1.38
		S.D.	3.66	3.72	
4.	Academic Adjustment	Mean	15.55	15.58	0.16
		S.D.	3.08	3.19	
5.	Health Adjustment	Mean	14.60	14.38	1.12
		S.D.	3.28	3.57	
6.	Total Adjustment	Mean	73.52	73.26	0.38
		S.D.	11.58	12.29	

Table 4.3. Marital Status and Adjustment (N= 1400)

	Dimensions	Mean & S.D.	Married (N=397)	Unmarried (N=1003)	t Values
1.	Home Adjustment	Mean	16.12	15.76	1.94
		S.D.	3.17	3.03	
2.	Social Adjustment	Mean	15.55	15.72	1.01
		S.D.	2.72	2.71	
3.	Emotional Adjustment	Mean	11.56	11.89	1.50
		S.D.	3.60	3.70	
4.	Academic Adjustment	Mean	15.63	15.53	0.57
		S.D.	3.26	3.05	
5.	Health Adjustment	Mean	14.52	14.55	0.11
		S.D.	3.50	3.32	
6.	Total Adjustment	Mean	73.41	73.46	0.07
		S.D.	12.46	11.52	

Comparison across Branch

The mean scores of adjustment dimensions across the Biological sciences, Physical sciences, Commerce and Arts faculty prospective teachers are presented in table-5. The comparison of the scores indicated that the four branches of prospective teachers differ statistically on health and total adjustment dimensions.

More specifically, it is observed that the differences are statistically significant across the health adjustment dimension ($f = 3.89$; $p < 0.01$) and total adjustment dimensions ($f = 3.60$; $p < 0.05$).

Comparison across Medium

The mean scores of adjustment dimensions across the English and Telugu medium prospective teachers are presented in table-6. The comparison of the scores indicated that the two mediums of prospective teachers differ statistically on social, emotional, academic, health and total adjustment dimensions.

Table 4.4. Educational Qualifications and Adjustment (N= 1400)

	Dimensions	Mean & S.D.	Graduation (N=1044)	Post graduation (N=356)	t Values
1.	Home Adjustment	Mean	16.02	15.42	3.15**
		S.D.	2.97	3.32	
2.	Social Adjustment	Mean	15.79	15.31	2.93**
		S.D.	2.54	3.12	
3.	Emotional Adjustment	Mean	11.74	11.97	1.02
		S.D.	3.64	3.77	
4.	Academic Adjustment	Mean	15.65	15.27	1.98*
		S.D.	3.06	3.26	
5.	Health Adjustment	Mean	14.59	14.40	0.91
		S.D.	3.30	3.55	
6.	Total Adjustment	Mean	73.81	72.39	1.96*
		S.D.	11.51	12.53	

**P < 0.01
*P < 0.05

More specifically, it is observed that the differences are statistically significant across the social adjustment dimension ($t = 5.15$; $p < 0.01$), emotional adjustment dimension ($t = 2.05$; $p < 0.05$), academic adjustment dimension ($t = 2.90$; $p < 0.01$), health adjustment dimension ($t = 2.53$; $p < 0.05$) and total adjustment dimension ($t = 2.48$; $p < 0.05$).

Comparison across Social Status

The mean scores of adjustment dimensions across the OC, BC, SC and ST community prospective teachers are presented in table-7. The comparison of the scores indicated that the four communities of prospective teachers differ statistically on home, social, academic and total adjustment dimensions.

Table 4.5. Branch and Adjustment
(N=1400)

	Dimensions	Mean& SD	Biological Sciences (N=302)	Physical Sciences (N=542)	Commerce (N=84)	Arts (N=472)	F values
1.	Home Adjustment	Mean	15.75	16.02	15.41	15.84	1.22
		SD	3.00	3.16	3.41	2.94	
2.	Social Adjustment	Mean	15.44	15.72	15.25	15.84	2.14
		SD	2.92	2.73	3.02	2.47	
3.	Emotional Adjustment	Mean	11.49	12.03	11.33	11.81	1.39
		SD	3.66	3.75	3.83	3.57	
4.	Academic Adjustment	Mean	15.29	15.65	14.94	15.72	2.46
		SD	3.15	3.09	3.47	3.03	
5.	Health Adjustment	Mean	14.35	14.82	13.58	14.51	3.89**
		SD	3.33	3.20	4.11	3.40	
6.	Total Adjustment	Mean	72.33	74.26	70.52	73.75	3.60*
		SD	11.17	12.23	13.06	11.32	

*$P < 0.05$
**$P < 0.01$

More specifically, it is observed that the differences are statistically significant across the home adjustment dimension ($f = 8.53$; $p < 0.01$), social adjustment dimensions ($f = 9.11$; $p < 0.01$), academic adjustment dimension ($f = 7.41$; $p < 0.01$) and total adjustment dimension ($f = 8.06$; $p < 0.01$).

Comparison across Native Area

The mean scores of adjustment dimensions in comparison across the native area i.e. rural, urban and agency areas are tabulated in the table-8. It can be observed that the home, social, academic and total adjustment dimensions obtained are statistically significant values. Where as, the other dimensions like emotional adjustment and health adjustment are not significant.

Table 4.6. Medium and Adjustment
(N= 1400)

	Dimensions	Mean & S.D.	English (N=184)	Telugu (N=1216)	t Values
1.	Home Adjustment	Mean	15.50	15.92	1.75
		S.D.	3.58	2.99	
2.	Social Adjustment	Mean	14.72	15.81	5.15**
		S.D.	3.41	2.56	
3.	Emotional Adjustment	Mean	12.32	11.72	2.05*
		S.D.	3.88	3.64	
4.	Academic Adjustment	Mean	14.94	15.65	2.90**
		S.D.	3.26	3.08	
5.	Health Adjustment	Mean	13.95	14.63	2.53*
		S.D.	3.62	3.32	
6.	Total Adjustment	Mean	71.44	73.75	2.48*
		S.D.	13.63	11.46	

**P < 0.01
*P < 0.05

More elaborately, the home adjustment (f = 6.76; p<0.01), social adjustment (f=18.37; p<0.01), academic adjustment (f=8.18; p<0.01) and total adjustment (f=9.54; p<0.01) are statistically significant in comparison across the native area i.e. rural, urban and agency area prospective teachers.

Comparison across District

The mean scores of adjustment dimensions in comparison across the district i.e. Srikakulam, Vizianagaram and Visakhapatnam districts are tabulated in the table-9. It can be observed that only the emotional adjustment dimension obtained is statistically significant value. Where as, the other dimensions like home, social, academic, health and total adjustments are not significant.

Table 4.7. Social Status and Adjustment (N=1400)

	Dimensions	Mean & S.D.	O.C. (N=236)	B.C. (N=744)	S.C. (N=300)	S.T. (N=120)	F Values
1.	Home Adjustment	Mean	16.25	15.97	15.81	14.60	8.53**
		SD	3.19	3.02	3.02	3.03	
2.	Social Adjustment	Mean	15.83	15.79	15.75	14.45	9.11**
		SD	2.60	2.60	2.78	3.13	
3.	Emotional Adjustment	Mean	11.83	11.93	11.76	11.03	2.07
		SD	3.95	3.53	3.69	3.92	
4.	Academic Adjustment	Mean	15.50	15.75	15.62	14.32	7.41**
		SD	3.29	3.06	3.01	3.06	
5.	Health Adjustment	Mean	14.37	14.63	14.65	14.05	1.30
		SD	3.44	3.34	3.47	3.13	
6.	Total Adjustment	Mean	73.80	74.08	73.60	68.46	8.06**
		SD	12.03	11.69	11.61	11.31	

**P < 0.01

More elaborately, the emotional adjustment (f = 5.57; p<0.01) is statistically significant in comparison across the Srikakulam, Vizianagaram and Visakhapatnam districts prospective teachers.

Comparison across Present Stay

The mean scores of adjustment dimensions in comparison across the present stay i.e. home, room and hostel resident prospective teachers are tabulated in the table-10. It can be observed that the home and academic adjustment dimensions obtained are statistically significant values. Where as, the other dimensions like social, emotional, health and total adjustments are not significant.

Table 4.8. Native Area and Adjustment (N=1400)

	Dimensions	Mean & S.D.	Rural l(N=887)	Urban (N=435)	Agency (N=78)	F-values
1.	Home Adjustment	Mean	15.91	16.00	14.64	6.76**
		SD	3.03	3.14	2.98	
2.	Social Adjustment	Mean	15.85	15.62	13.93	18.37**
		SD	2.62	2.62	3.49	
3.	Emotional Adjustment	Mean	11.78	11.95	11.17	1.51
		SD	3.65	3.70	3.77	
4.	Academic Adjustment	Mean	15.61	15.70	14.19	8.18**
		SD	3.11	3.06	3.12	
5.	Health Adjustment	Mean	14.59	14.55	13.87	1.66
		SD	3.31	3.51	3.19	
6.	Total Adjustment	Mean	73.75	73.84	67.82	9.54**
		SD	11.57	11.98	11.94	

**P < 0.01

Table 4.9. District And Adjustment (N=1400)

	Dimensions	Mean & S.D.	Srika-kulam (N=510)	Viziana-garam (N=450)	Visakha-patnam (N=440)	F-values
1.	Home Adjustment	Mean	15.81	15.86	15.93	0.20
		SD	3.04	3.25	2.92	
2.	Social Adjustment	Mean	15.75	15.57	15.68	0.49
		SD	2.74	2.76	2.62	
3.	Emotional Adjustment	Mean	11.43	11.79	12.23	5.57**
		SD	3.50	3.69	3.83	
4.	Academic Adjustment	Mean	15.35	15.74	15.61	1.91
		SD	3.22	3.17	2.92	
5.	Health Adjustment	Mean	14.46	14.59	14.58	0.22
		SD	3.47	3.23	3.39	
6.	Total Adjustment	Mean	72.82	73.57	74.05	1.33
		SD	12.05	11.90	11.36	

**P < 0.01

More elaborately, the home adjustment (f = 3.96; p<0.05) and academic adjustment (f=3.55; p<0.05) dimensions are statistically significant in comparison across the present stay i.e. home, room and hostel resident prospective teachers.

Comparison across Parental Education:

The mean scores of adjustment dimensions in comparison across the parental education i.e. both parents are educated, one parent educated and both parents are un-educated of prospective teachers are tabulated in the table-11. It can be observed that only the home adjustment dimension obtained is statistically significant value. Where as, the other dimensions like social, emotional, academic, health and total adjustments are not significant.

More elaborately, the home adjustment (f = 7.84; p<0.01) dimension is statistically significant in comparison across the parental education i.e. both parents are educated, one parent educated and both parents are un-educated of prospective teachers

Table 4.10. Present Stay and Adjustment (N=1400)

	Dimensions	Mean & S.D.	Home (N=947)	Room (N=287)	Hostel (N=166)	F-values
1.	Home Adjustment	Mean	16.02	15.51	15.57	3.96*
		SD	3.10	2.91	3.13	
2.	Social Adjustment	Mean	15.76	15.47	15.54	1.49
		SD	2.56	2.94	3.08	
3.	Emotional Adjustment	Mean	11.83	11.52	12.10	1.36
		SD	3.63	3.71	3.89	
4.	Academic Adjustment	Mean	15.69	15.13	15.51	3.55*
		SD	3.04	3.13	3.41	
5.	Health Adjustment	Mean	14.54	14.48	14.64	0.11
		SD	3.42	3.37	3.04	
6.	Total Adjustment	Mean	73.36	72.14	73.37	2.34
		SD	11.57	11.84	12.82	

**P < 0.05

Table 4.11. Parental Education And Adjustment (N=1400)

	Dimensions	Mean & S.D.	Both educated (N=473)	One educated (N=526)	Both un-educated (N=401)	F-values
1.	Home Adjustment	Mean	16.27	15.81	15.46	7.84**
		SD	3.12	3.04	3.01	
2.	Social Adjustment	Mean	15.70	15.59	15.74	0.36
		SD	2.64	2.65	2.87	
3.	Emotional Adjustment	Mean	11.87	11.69	11.86	0.37
		SD	3.55	3.77	3.70	
4.	Academic Adjustment	Mean	15.74	15.57	15.32	1.94
		SD	3.12	3.04	3.19	
5.	Health Adjustment	Mean	14.51	14.54	14.58	0.04
		SD	3.56	3.28	3.26	
6.	Total Adjustment	Mean	74.10	73.22	72.97	1.16
		SD	12.04	11.44	11.93	

** P < 0.01

Comparison across Teaching Parents

The mean scores of adjustment dimensions across the teaching parents of prospective teachers are presented in table-12. The comparison of the scores indicated that the four groups i.e. both parents are teachers, father teacher, Mother teacher, parents working in other than teacher jobs of prospective teachers differ statistically on home, social, academic, health and total adjustment dimensions.

More specifically, it is observed that the differences are statistically significant across the home adjustment dimension ($f = 5.83$; $p < 0.01$), social adjustment dimension ($f = 6.59$; $p < 0.01$), academic adjustment dimension ($f = 6.22$; $p < 0.01$), health adjustment dimension ($f = 4.71$; $p < 0.01$) and total adjustment dimension ($f = 7.68$; $p < 0.01$).

Comparison across Parental Professions

The mean scores of adjustment dimensions across the parental professions of prospective teachers are presented in table-13. The comparison of the scores indicated that the four groups i.e. agricultural parents, parents working in private jobs, parents working in government jobs and business parents of prospective teachers differ statistically on social adjustment dimension.

More specifically, it is observed that the differences are statistically significant across the social adjustment dimension (f = 4.86; p < 0.01).

Table 4.12. Teaching Parents and Adjustment (N=1400)

	Dimensions	Mean & S.D.	Both teachers (N=24)	Father teacher (N=130)	Mother teacher (N=20)	Other jobs (N=1226)	F values
1.	Home Adjustment	Mean	13.66	15.34	15.95	15.96	5.83**
		SD	4.71	3.99	3.61	2.89	
2.	Social Adjustment	Mean	13.79	15.17	14.85	15.77	6.59**
		SD	4.20	3.06	3.09	2.61	
3.	Emotional Adjustment	Mean	10.45	11.56	13.25	11.82	2.29
		SD	3.03	3.42	3.27	3.71	
4.	Academic Adjustment	Mean	13.37	14.94	15.40	15.67	6.22**
		SD	4.30	3.67	3.01	3.00	
5.	Health Adjustment	Mean	12.70	13.99	13.45	14.65	4.71**
		SD	4.21	3.79	3.48	3.28	
6.	Total Adjustment	Mean	64.00	71.03	72.90	73.90	7.68**
		SD	17.30	14.32	12.43	11.25	

**P < 0.01

Comparison across Monthly Family Income

The analysis of the data involved the comparison of the adjustment variables across the monthly family income i.e. below Rs 5,000, between Rs 5,000 to Rs 10,000, between Rs

10,000 to Rs 20,000 and above Rs 20,000. The mean scores and F-values are tabulated in table-14. It can be observed that the F-values obtained across the four groups are not significant.

Table 4.13. Parental Processions and Adjustment (N=1400)

	Dimensions	Mean & S.D.	Agricul. (N=619)	Private jobs (N=227)	Govt. jobs (N=457)	Business (N=97)	F values
1.	Home Adjustment	Mean	15.78	15.71	16.02	16.04	0.80**
		SD	2.81	3.26	3.31	3.04	
2.	Social Adjustment	Mean	15.87	15.07	15.67	15.77	4.86**
		SD	2.67	3.06	2.61	2.39	
3.	Emotional Adjustment	Mean	11.85	11.95	11.80	11.07	1.44
		SD	3.56	3.81	3.75	3.71	
4.	Academic Adjustment	Mean	15.61	15.50	15.57	15.24	0.42**
		SD	3.07	3.23	3.10	3.18	
5.	Health Adjustment	Mean	14.68	14.57	14.41	14.17	0.96**
		SD	3.12	3.19	3.65	3.86	
6.	Total Adjustment	Mean	73.81	72.83	73.50	72.30	0.71**
		SD	11.06	12.32	12.48	11.76	

**P < 0.01

Comparison across Type of Family

The mean scores of adjustment dimensions across the nuclear and joint family prospective teachers are tabulated in table-15. The comparison of the scores indicated that the two family groups of prospective teachers differ statistically on social adjustment dimension.

More specifically, the statistical significant difference was observed for the social adjustment dimension ($t = 2.22$; $p < 0.05$).

Table 4.14. Monthly Family Income And Adjustment (N=1400)

	Dimensions	Mean & S.D.	Below Rs. 5000 (N=424)	Rs. 5000 Rs. 10000 (N=659)	Rs. 10000 Rs. 20000 (N=243)	Above Rs. 20000 (N=74)	F values
1.	Home Adjustment	Mean	15.79	15.76	16.20	16.13	1.45
		SD	2.88	3.21	3.02	3.08	
2.	Social Adjustment	Mean	15.75	15.54	15.94	15.55	1.46
		SD	2.76	2.77	2.59	2:22	
3.	Emotional Adjustment	Mean	11.59	11.79	12.04	12.25	1.16
		SD	3.74	3.66	3.75	3.13	
4.	Academic Adjustment	Mean	15.56	15.54	15.65	15.44	0.11
		SD	3.01	3.11	3.33	3.01	
5.	Health Adjustment	Mean	14.54	14.53	14.65	14.25	0.26
		SD	3.07	3.41	3.65	3.69	
6.	Total Adjustment	Mean	73.25	73.7	74.48	73.64	0.79
		SD	11.20	11.95	12.52	11.19	

Table 4.15. Type of Family and Adjustment (N= 1400)

	Dimensions	Mean & S.D.	Nuclear (N=874)	Joint (N=526)	t Values
1.	Home Adjustment	Mean	15.95	15.73	1.32
		S.D.	3.06	3.09	
2.	Social Adjustment	Mean	15.80	15.46	2.22*
		S.D.	2.61	2.86	
3.	Emotional Adjustment	Mean	11.66	12.02	1.79
		S.D.	3.73	3.58	
4.	Academic Adjustment	Mean	15.56	15.55	0.05
		S.D.	3.09	3.15	
5.	Health Adjustment	Mean	14.60	14.44	0.84
		S.D.	3.38	3.36	
6.	Total Adjustment	Mean	73.58	73.22	0.55
		S.D.	11.73	11.89	

**P < 0.05

SECTION-II

Interaction Effects

This section includes the results regarding the gender interactions of adjustments on individual variables like age, marital status, educational qualifications, branch, medium, social status, native area, district, present stay, parental education, teaching parents, parental professions, monthly family income and type of family.

The prospective teachers include both male and female student teachers. The independent variable gender categorized by male and female and this variable is again categorized the sub-groups of each individual dimension of age, marital status, educational qualifications, branch, medium, social status, native area, district, present stay, parental education, teaching parents, parental professions, monthly family income and type of family. This study can deeply measure the each dimension of adjustment across the individual variables. It also explains the impact of adjustment on various variables.

The adjustment scores measures the degree of adjustment in prospective teachers. The higher mean scores indicate the degree of adjustment in the respective dimensions.

Interaction of Age and Gender

The analysis of the data involved the interaction of the age and gender on adjustment factors. The mean scores and F-values are tabulated in table-16. It can be observed that all the adjustment dimensions are statistically non-significant.

Interaction of Marital Status and Gender

The analysis of the data involved the interaction of the marital status and gender on adjustment factors. The mean scores and F-values are tabulated in table-17. It can be observed that all the adjustment dimensions are statistically non-significant.

Table 4.16. Interaction of Age and Gender on Adjustment Factors (N=1400)

Dimensions	Age	Below 25 Years (N=993)		Aboye 25years (N=407)		
	Gender	Male (N=331)	Female (N=662)	Male (N=175)	Female (N=232)	F-values
Home adjustment	Mean	15.30	16.20	15.13	16.28	0.37
	S.D.	2.98	2.93	3.42	3.13	
Social adjustment	Mean	15.93	15.66	15.61	15.39	2.71
	S.D.	2.82	2.68	2.72	2.61	
Emotional adjustment	Mean	12.16	11.48	12.53	11.62	1.92
	S.D.	3.73	3.60	3.85	3.58	
Academic adjustment	Mean	15.33	15.66	15.61	15.56	0.02
	S.D.	3.24	2.99	3.16	3.22	
Health adjustment	Mean	14.51	14.65	14.60	14.21	1.25
	S.D.	3.40	3.22	3.38	3.70	
Total adjustment	Mean	73.25	73.66	73.50	73.08	0.14
	S.D.	12.34	11.19	12.34	12.29	

* $P < 0.05$
** $P < 0.01$

Interaction of Educational Qualifications and Gender

The analysis of the data involved the interaction of educational qualifications and gender on adjustment factors. The mean scores and F-values are tabulated in table-18. It can be observed that the home, social, academic and total adjustment dimensions are statistically significant.

More specifically, it is observed that the differences are statistically significant across the home adjustment dimension (f = 9.95; $p < 0.01$), social adjustment (f=8.62; $P<0.01$), academic adjustment dimension (f=3.95; $P<0.05$) and total adjustment dimension (f = 3.85; $p < 0.05$).

Interaction of Branch and Gender

The analysis of the data involved the interaction of branch and gender on adjustment factors. The mean scores and F-values are tabulated in table-19. It can be observed that the health and total adjustment dimensions are statistically significant.

Table 4.17. Interaction of Marital Status and Gender on Adjustment Factors (N=1400)

Dimensions	Marital Status	Married (N=397)		Un-married (N=1003)		F-values
	Gender	Male (N=64)	Female (N=333)	Male (N=442)	Female (N=561)	
Home adjustment	Mean	14.57	16.42	15.34	16.10	3.76
	S.D.	3.81	2.95	3.02	3.00	
Social adjustment	Mean	15.21	15.62	15.90	15.57	1.02
	S.D.	3.37	2.57	2.69	2.72	
Emotional adjustment	Mean	12.48	11.39	12.26	11.60	2.25
	S.D.	3.75	3.55	3.78	3.62	
Academic adjustment	Mean	15.07	15.74	15.47	15.57	0.32
	S.D.	3.43	3.22	3.18	2.95	
Health adjustment	Mean	14.12	14.60	14.61	14.50	0.01
	S.D.	3.70	3.46	3.34	3.30	
Total adjustment	Mean	71.48	73.78	73.61	73.35	0.006
	S.D.	14.34	12.05	12.00	11.14	

* $P < 0.05$
** $P < 0.01$

More specifically, it is observed that the differences are statistically significant across the health adjustment dimension (f = 3.89; p < 0.05) and total adjustment dimension (f = 3.60; p < 0.05).

Table 4.18. Interaction of Educational Qualifications and Gender on Adjustment Factors (N=1400)

Dimensions	Education	Graduation (N=1044)		Post-graduation (N=356)		
	Gender	Male (N=343)	Female (N=701)	Male (N=163)	Female (N=193)	F-values
Home adjustment	Mean	15.47	16.28	14.76	15.98	9.95**
	S.D.	3.02	2.91	3.33	3.22	
Social adjustment	Mean	16.04	15.68	15.35	15.27	8.62**
	S.D.	2.56	2.53	3.17	3.09	
Emotional adjustment	Mean	12.32	11.45	12.22	11.76	1.05
	S.D.	3.65	3.61	4.04	3.52	
Academic adjustment	Mean	15.53	15.71	15.19	15.34	3.95*
	S.D.	3.17	3.00	3.31	3.23	
Health adjustment	Mean	14.62	14.57	14.38	14.41	0.84
	S.D.	3.29	3.31	3.59	3.52	
Total adjustment	Mean	74.01	73.71	71.92	72.78	3.85*
	S.D.	11.76	11.39	13.36	11.80	

* P < 0.05
** P < 0.01

Interaction of Medium and Gender

The analysis of the data involved the interaction of medium of instruction and gender on adjustment factors. The mean scores and F-values are tabulated in table-20. It can be observed that the social, emotional, academic, health and total adjustment dimensions are statistically significant.

Table 4.19. Interaction of Branch and Gender on Adjustment Factors (N=1400)

Dimensions	Branch	Biological Sciences (N=302)		Physical Sciences (N=542)		Commerce (N=84)		Arts Subjects (N=472)		F-values
	Gender	Male (N=93)	Female (N=209)	Male (N=202)	Female (N=340)	Male (N=27)	Female (N=57)	Male (N=184)	Female (N=288)	
Home adjustment	Mean	15.61	15.81	15.37	16.41	13.96	16.10	15.11	16.31	1.22
	S.D.	2.70	3.13	3.32	3.01	3.52	3.16	3.05	2.78	
Social adjustment	Mean	15.82	15.26	15.86	15.63	14.11	15.78	16.02	15.73	2.14
	S.D.	2.58	3.05	2.86	2.65	3.66	2.53	2.59	2.39	
Emotional adjustment	Mean	12.01	11.26	12.24	11.91	11.77	11.12	12.57	11.32	1.89
	S.D.	3.60	3.67	4.11	3.51	4.07	3.73	3.42	3.58	
Academic adjustment	Mean	15.43	15.23	15.34	15.84	14.44	15.17	15.66	15.76	2.46
	S.D.	2.90	3.26	3.42	2.87	3.68	3.38	3.04	3.02	
Health adjustment	Mean	14.66	14.21	14.68	14.90	12.74	13.98	14.60	14.45	3.89*
	S.D.	3.18	3.40	3.41	3.07	4.71	3.78	3.19	3.39	
Total adjustment	Mean	73.54	71.79	73.50	74.72	67.03	72.17	73.98	73.60	3.60*
	S.D.	10.56	11.42	13.33	11.52	14.76	11.95	11.44	11.26	

* $P < 0.05$
** $P < 0.01$

More specifically, it is observed that the differences are statistically significant across the social adjustment dimension ($f = 26.56; p < 0.01$), emotional adjustment ($f=4.22; P< 0.05$), academic adjustment dimension ($f=8.45; P< 0.01$), health adjustment dimension ($f = 6.44; p < 0.05$) and total adjustment dimension ($f = 6.18; p < 0.05$).

Interaction of Social Status and Gender

The analysis of the data involved the interaction of social status and gender on adjustment factors. The mean scores and F-values are tabulated in table-21. It can be observed that the home, social, academic and total adjustment dimensions are statistically significant.

Table 4.20. Interaction of Medium and Gender on Adjustment Factors (N=1400)

Dimensions	Medium	English (N=184)		Telugu (N=1216)		
	Gender	Male (N=53)	Female (N=131)	Male (N=453)	Female (N=763)	F-values
Home adjustment	Mean	15.47	16.28	14.76	15.98	9.95**
	S.D.	3.02	2.91	3.33	3.22	
Social adjustment	Mean	16.04	15.68	15.35	15.27	8.62**
	S.D.	2.56	2.53	3.17	3.09	
Emotional adjustment	Mean	12.32	11.45	12.22	11.76	1.05
	S.D.	3.65	3.61	4.04	3.52	
Academic adjustment	Mean	15.53	15.71	15.19	15.34	3.95*
	S.D.	3.17	3.00	3.31	3.23	
Health adjustment	Mean	14.62	14.57	14.38	14.41	0.84
	S.D.	3.29	3.31	3.59	3.52	
Total adjustment	Mean	74.01	73.71	71.92	72.78	3.85*
	S.D.	11.76	11.39	13.36	11.80	

*P < 0.05
**P < 0.01

Table 4.21. Interaction of Social Status and Gender on Adjustment Factors (N=1400)

Dimensions	Social Status	OC (N=236)		BC (N=744)		SC (N=300)		ST (N=120)		
	Gender	Male (N=38)	Female (N=198)	Male (N=252)	Female (N=492)	Male (N=140)	Female (N=160)	Male (N=76)	Female (N=44)	F-values
Home adjustment	Mean	1413	16.66	15.57	16.17	15.39	16.17	14.43	14.88	8.53**
	S.D.	4.31	2.76	3.03	2.99	2.91	3.07	3.00	3.09	
Social adjustment	Mean	15.05	15.98	16.18	15.58	15.93	15.59	14.78	13.86	9.11**
	S.D.	3.01	2.49	2.52	2.61	2.92	2.66	2.98	3.33	
Emotional adjustment	Mean	11.92	11.82	2.78	11.49	12.09	11.46	11.22	10.70	2.07
	S.D.	4.78	3.78	3.70	3.36	3.52	3.82	3.70	4.30	
Academic adjustment	Mean	14.81	15.63	15.72	15.77	15.64	15.61	14.36	14.25	7.41**
	S.D.	3.89	3.16	3.31	2.93	2.86	3.15	2.92	3.33	
Health adjustment	Mean	13.65	14.51	14.70	14.59	14.80	14.53	14.02	14.11	1.30
	S.D.	4.33	3.24	3.44	3.29	3.07	3.78	3.20	3.03	
Total adjustment	Mean	69.57	74.62	74.97	73.62	73.86	73.38	68.84	67.81	8.06**
	S.D.	15.79	11.03	12.42	11.29	11.08	12.09	10.91	12.06	

* $P < 0.05$
** $P < 0.01$

More specifically, it is observed that the differences are statistically significant across the home adjustment dimension ($f = 8.53$; $p < 0.01$), social adjustment ($f = 9.11$; $P < 0.01$), academic adjustment dimension ($f = 7.41$; $P < 0.01$) and total adjustment dimension ($f = 8.06$; $p < 0.01$).

Interaction of Native Area and Gender

The analysis of the data involved the interaction of native area and gender on adjustment factors. The mean scores and F-values are tabulated in table-22. It can be observed that the home, social, academic and total adjustment dimensions are statistically significant.

More specifically, it is observed that the differences are statistically significant across the home adjustment dimension ($f=6.76$; $p < 0.01$), social adjustment ($f=18.37$; $P < 0.01$), academic adjustment dimension ($f=8.18$; $P < 0.01$) and total adjustment dimension ($f = 9.54$; $p < 0.01$).

Interaction of District and Gender

The analysis of the data involved the interaction of district and gender on adjustment factors. The mean scores and F-values are tabulated in table-23. It can be observed that only the emotional adjustment dimension is statistically significant.

More specifically, it is observed that the differences are statistically significant across the emotional adjustment dimension ($f = 5.57$; $p < 0.01$).

Interaction of Present Stay and Gender

The analysis of the data involved the interaction of present stay and gender on adjustment factors. The mean scores and F-values are tabulated in table-24. It can be observed that the home and academic adjustment dimensions are statistically significant.

More specifically, it is observed that the differences are statistically significant across the home adjustment

Table 4.22. Interaction of Native Area and Gender on Adjustment Factors (N=1400)

Dimensions	Native area	Rural (N=887)		Urban (N=435)		Agency (N=78)		F- values
	Gender	Male (N=356)	Female (N=531)	Male (N=98)	Female (N=337)	Male (N=52)	Female (N=26)	
Home adjustment	Mean	15.48	16.19	14.83	16.34	14.36	15.19	6.76**
	S.D.	3.01	3.01	3.61	2.91	2.81	3.27	
Social adjustment	Mean	16.23	15.59	15.27	15.73	14.00	13.80	18.37**
	S.D.	2.47	2.70	2.92	2.52	3.64	3.24	
Emotional adjustment	Mean	12.44	11.33	12.28	11.86	11.28	10.96	1.51
	S.D.	3.70	3.56	4.00	3.61	3.71	3.95	
Academic adjustment	Mean	15.71	15.53	14.95	15.92	14.32	13.92	8.18**
	S.D.	3.15	3.08	3.43	2.92	2.92	3.53	
Health adjustment	Mean	14.83	14.44	14.05	14.69	13.55	14.50	1.66
	S.D.	3.25	3.34	3.81	3.42	3.28	2.96	
Total adjustment	Mean	74.72	73.10	71.40	74.55	67.53	68.38	9.54**
	S.D.	11.63	11.49	13.93	11.27	11.77	12.49	

*P < 0.05
**P < 0.01

Table 4.23. Interaction of District and Gender on Adjustment Factors (N=1400)

Dimensions	District	Srikakulam (N=510)		Viziangaram (N=450)		Visakhapatnam (N=440)		F-values
	Gender	Male (N=181)	Female (N=329)	Male (N=169)	Female (N=281)	Male (N=156)	Female (N=284)	
Home adjustment	Mean	14.98	16.26	15.42	16.13	15.35	16.25	0.20
	S.D.	3.11	2.91	3.25	3.23	3.05	2.81	
Social adjustment	Mean	15.59	15.83	15.79	15.44	16.11	15.45	0.49
	S.D.	3.00	2.59	2.73	2.77	2.57	2.63	
Emotional adjustment	Mean	11.97	11.13	12.45	11.39	12.48	12.09	5.57**
	S.D.	3.72	3.34	3.87	3.52	3.74	3.88	
Academic adjustment	Mean	15.13	15.47	15.58	15.83	15.59	15.62	1.91
	S.D.	3.38	3.12	3.14	3.18	3.09	2.83	
Health adjustment	Mean	14.38	14.51	14.50	14.64	14.79	14.46	0.22
	S.D.	3.59	3.40	3.42	3.13	3.12	3.53	
Total adjustment	Mean	72.07	73.23	73.76	73.45	74.35	73.89	1.33
	S.D.	13.02	11.48	12.26	11.70	11.50	11.30	

*P < 0.05
**P < 0.01

dimension ($f = 3.96$; $p < 0.05$) and academic adjustment dimension ($f=3.55$; $P< 0.05$).

Interaction of Parental Education and Gender

The analysis of the data involved the interaction of parental education and gender on adjustment factors. The mean scores and F-values are tabulated in table-25. It can be observed that only the home adjustment dimension is statistically significant.

More specifically, it is observed that the differences are statistically significant across the home adjustment dimension ($f = 7.84$; $p < 0.01$).

Interaction of Teaching Parents and Gender

The analysis of the data involved the interaction of teaching parents and gender on adjustment factors. The mean scores and F-values are tabulated in table-26. It can be observed that the home, social, academic, health and total adjustment dimensions are statistically significant.

More specifically, it is observed that the differences are statistically significant across the home adjustment dimension ($f = 5.83$; $p < 0.01$), social adjustment ($f=6.59$; $P< 0.01$), academic adjustment dimension ($f=6.22$; $P< 0.01$), health adjustment dimension ($f = 4.71$; $p < 0.05$) and total adjustment dimension ($f = 7.68$; $p < 0.05$).

Interaction of Parental Professions and Gender

The analysis of the data involved the interaction of parental professions and gender on adjustment factors. The mean scores and F-values are tabulated in table-27. It can be observed that only the social adjustment dimension is statistically significant.

More specifically, it is observed that the differences are statistically significant across the social adjustment dimension ($f = 4.86$; $p < 0.01$).

Table 4.24. Interaction of Present Stay and Gender on Adjustment Factors (N=1400)

Dimensions	Present Stay	Home (N=947)		Room (N=287)		Hostel (N=166)		F-values
	Gender	Male (N=238)	Female (N=709)	Male (N=178)	Female (N=109)	Male (N=90)	Female (N=76)	
Home adjustment	Mean	15.21	16.30	15.26	15.91	15.27	15.92	3.96 *
	S.D.	3.34	2.97	2.89	2.90	3.09	3.18	
Social adjustment	Mean	15.89	15.71	15.76	14.98	15.73	15.31	1.49
	S.D.	2.68	2.52	2.80	3.11	3.07	3.10	
Emotional adjustment	Mean	12.62	11.56	11.98	10.78	12.04	12.17	1.36
	S.D.	3.95	3.48	3.51	3.91	3.77	4.05	
Academic adjustment	Mean	15.50	15.76	15.36	14.77	15.34	15.72	3.55 *
	S.D.	3.14	3.01	3.15	3.08	3.54	3.26	
Health adjustment	Mean	14.52	14.55	14.51	14.44	14.70	14.57	0.11
	S.D.	3.54	3.38	3.43	3.29	2.90	3.23	
Total adjustment	Mean	73.76	73.89	72.89	70.90	73.10	73.71	2.34
	S.D.	12.71	11.16	11.72	11.99	12.55	13.21	

* $P < 0.05$
** $P < 0.01$

Table 4.25. Interaction of Parental Education and Gender on Adjustment Factors (N=1400)

Dimensions	Parents Education	Both are educated (N=473)		One parent educated (N=526)		Both are un-educated (N=401)		F-values
	Gender	Male (N=78)	Female (N=395)	Male (N=174)	Female (N=352)	Male (N=254)	Female (N=147)	
Home adjustment	Means	14.83	16.56	15.39	16.01	15.27	15.78	7.84**
	S.D.	3.69	2.92	3.07	3.01	3.00	3.00	
Social adjustment	Mean	15.37	15.76	15.88	15.45	15.91	15.44	0.36
	S.D.	2.57	2.65	2.67	2.64	2.92	2.75	
Emotional adjustment	Mean	12.19	11.80	12.35	11.36	12.28	11.12	0.37
	S.D.	3.86	3.49	3.87	3.68	3.69	3.62	
Academic adjustment	Mean	15.52	15.78	15.60	15.56	15.27	15.40	1.94
	S.D.	3.29	3.09	3.00	3.06	3.34	2.94	
Health adjustment	Mean	13.75	14.66	14.70	14.46	14.68	14.40	0.04
	S.D.	3.98	3.46	3.25	3.29	3.26	3.25	
Total adjustment	Mean	71.67	74.58	73.93	72.86	73.44	72.17	1.16
	S.D.	13.74	11.63	11.62	11.35	12.35	11.19	

*P < 0.05
**P < 0.01

Table 4.26. Interaction of Teaching Parents and Gender on Adjustment Factors (N=1400)

Dimensions	Parents profession	Both are teachers (N=24)		Father teacher (N=130)		Mother teacher (N=20)		Other Jobs (N=1226)		
	Gender	Male (N=5)	Female (N=19)	Male (N=24)	Female (N=106)	Male (N=4)	Female (N=16)	Male (N=473)	Female (N=753)	F-values
Home adjustment	Mean	11.20	14.31	13.58	15.74	12.00	16.93	15.40	16.32	5.83**
	S.D.	4.65	4.63	4.17	3.85	4.08	2.83	2.99	2.77	
Social adjustment	Mean	14.20	13.68	14.66	15.29	13.00	15.31	15.92	15.68	6.59**
	S.D.	2.16	4.63	3.37	2.99	4.24	2.72	2.73	2.53	
Emotional adjustment	Mean	10.60	10.42	11.70	11.53	12.25	13.50	12.34	11.50	2.29
	S.D.	3.84	2.91	3.85	3.33	4.03	3.16	3.77	3.64	
Academic adjustment	Mean	12.60	13.57	14.29	15.09	14.75	15.56	15.52	15.76	6.22**
	S.D.	4.39	4.37	3.95	3.61	3.40	3.01	3.15	2.91	
Health adjustment	Mean	12.20	12.84	13.25	14.16	10.00	14.31	14.67	14.64	4.71**
	S.D.	4.86	4.16	3.59	3.84	3.16	3.07	3.33	3.26	
Total adjustment	Mean	60.80	64.84	67.50	71.83	62.00	75.62	73.86	73.92	7.68**
	S.D.	15.44	18.05	15.64	13.96	14.46	10.69	11.94	10.80	

* $P < 0.05$
** $P < 0.01$

Table 4.27. Interaction of Parental Professions and Gender on Adjustment Factors (N=1400)

Dimensions	Financial source	Agriculture (N=619)		Private jobs (N=227)		Government jobs (N=457)		Business (N=97)		
	Gender	Male (N=349)	Female (N=270)	Male (N=57)	Female (N=170)	Male (N=82)	Female (N=375)	Male (N=18)	Female (N=79)	F-values
Home adjustment	Mean	15.56	16.07	15.03	15.94	14.40	16.37	13.55	16.60	0.80
	S.D.	2.78	2.84	3.42	3.18	4.03	3.03	3.16	2.72	
Social adjustment	Mean	16.02	15.68	15.54	14.92	15.43	15.73	14.55	16.05	4.86**
	S.D.	2.69	2.64	2.95	3.08	3.02	2.51	2.66	2.25	
Emotional adjustment	Mean	12.41	11.13	12.64	11.71	12.21	11.72	9.22	11.49	1.44
	S.D.	3.57	3.42	3.75	3.82	4.36	3.60	3.70	3.60	
Academic adjustment	Mean	15.59	15.64	15.66	15.45	15.08	15.68	13.00	15.75	0.42
	S.D.	3.11	3.03	3.19	3.25	3.37	3.03	3.78	2.82	
Health adjustment	Mean	14.77	14.56	14.78	14.50	13.87	14.53	12.44	14.56	0.96
	S.D.	3.19	3.04	3.30	3.15	3.82	3.61	4.43	3.63	
Total adjustment	Mean	74.37	73.10	73.68	72.54	71.02	74.04	62.77	74.48	0.71
	S.D.	11.42	10.54	12.08	12.43	14.76	11.87	12.51	10.51	

* P < 0.05
** P < 0.01

Table 4.28. Interaction of Monthly Income and Gender on Adjustment Factors (N=1400)

Dimensions	Monthly source	Below Rs. 5000 (N=424)		Rs. 5000 to 10000 (N=659)		Rs. 10000 to 20000 (N=243)		Above Rs. 20000 (N=74)		
	Gender	Male (N=182)	Female (N=242)	Male (N=234)	Female (N=425)	Male (N=71)	Female (N=172)	Male (N=19)	Female (N=55)	F-values
Home adjustment	Mean	15.38	16.10	15.19	16.08	15.11	16.65	15.10	16.49	1.45
	S.D.	2.94	2.79	3.26	3.14	3.11	2.87	3.66	2.80	
Social adjustment	Mean	15.78	15.72	15.89	15.34	15.77	16.01	15.42	15.60	1.46
	S.D.	2.92	2.64	2.78	2.74	2.57	2.60	2.50	2.14	
Emotional adjustment	Mean	12.24	11.11	12.08	11.62	12.76	11.75	13.57	11.80	1.16
	S.D.	3.75	3.67	3.86	3.54	3.64	3.77	3.32	2.95	
Academic adjustment	Mean	15.34	15.72	15.51	15.55	15.29	15.79	15.63	15.38	0.11
	S.D.	3.01	3.01	3.32	2.99	3.46	3.28	3.04	3.02	
Health adjustment	Mean	14.50	14.58	14.40	14.60	15.18	14.43	14.36	14.21	0.26
	S.D.	3.14	3.03	3.50	3.36	3.57	3.66	3.63	3.74	
Total adjustment	Mean	73.26	73.25	73.10	73.21	74.12	74.63	74.10	73.49	0.79
	S.D.	11.79	10.75	12.66	11.56	12.71	12.47	12.49	10.83	

* $P < 0.05$
** $P < 0.01$

Table 4.29. Interaction of Type of Family and Gender on Adjustment Factors (N=1400)

Dimensions	Type of family	Nuclear family (N=874)		Joint family (N=526)		
	Gender	Male (N=262)	Female (N=612)	Male (N=244)	Female (N=282)	F-values
Home adjustment	Mean	15.13	16.30	15.36	16.04	1.74
	S.D.	3.31	2.88	2.94	3.19	
Social adjustment	Mean	15.96	15.73	15.67	15.29	4.96*
	S.D.	2.70	2.57	2.88	2.84	
Emotional adjustment	Mean	11.91	11.55	12.69	11.45	3.21
	S.D.	4.00	3.60	3.47	3.58	
Academic adjustment	Mean	15.16	15.73	15.70	15.42	0.003
	S.D.	3.36	2.96	3.03	3.24	
Health adjustment	Mean	14.53	14.63	14.56	14.33	0.72
	S.D.	3.50	3.33	3.28	3.42	
Total adjustment	Mean	72.71	73.96	74.01	72.54	0.30
	S.D.	13.13	11.07	11.39	12.29	

*P < 0.05
**P < 0.01

Interaction of Monthly Family Income and Gender

The analysis of the data involved the interaction of the monthly family income and gender on adjustment factors. The mean scores and F-values are tabulated in table-28. It can be observed that all the adjustment dimensions are statistically non-significant.

Interaction of Type of Family and Gender

The analysis of the data involved the interaction of type of family and gender on adjustment factors. The mean scores and F-values are tabulated in table-29. It can be observed that only the social adjustment dimension is statistically significant.

More specifically, it is observed that the differences are statistically significant across the social adjustment dimension ($f = 4.96$; $p < 0.05$).

SECTION III

CORRELATIONAL ANALYSES

This section includes the results regarding the relationships between the adjustment variables. The objective of the correlation analysis is to examine the relationship between adjustment dimensions. The hypothesis constructed for this, is the positive adjustment factors leads to better environmental adjustment.

Inter-Correlation Matrix of Adjustment Dimensions

The inter correlations between the variables of adjustment are presented in table-30. It can be noted that all the dependent variables are significantly and positively correlated between them. These correlations indicate that if one dimension adjusted better than the degree of adjustment increases between other dimensions.

Summery of the Results

The significant results were specifically mentioned and the non-significant results were noted in this chapter. The tables will clearly exhibit the significant differences and the degree of adjustments in the dimensions. The discussion related to the results will be followed in the next chapter.

Table 4.30. Inter-correlation Matrix of Adjustment Dimensions (N=1400)

Dimensions	Social Adjust-ment	Emotional Adjust-ment	Academic Adjust-ment	Health Adjust-ment	Total Adjust-ment
Home Adjustment	0.42**	0.37**	0.57**	0.47**	0.76**
Social Adjustment		0.19**	0.46**	0.31**	0.61**
Emotional Adjustment			0.48**	0.47**	0.72**
Academic Adjustment				0.49**	0.81**
Health Adjustment					0.76**

**P < 0.01

The discussion of the results of the present study is given in this chapter. The results are discussed according to the outcomes of the tables. The discussions are categorized into three sections of the following pages.

Section I includes the discussion related to the influence of individual variables on adjustment dimensions.

Section ll includes the discussion related to the gender interactions of individual variables on adjustment variables.

Section lII includes the discussion related to the relationships between different adjustment variables.

SECTION I
ADJUSTMENT DIMENSIONS

The discussion of results regarding the influence of each of the individual variables i.e. sex, age, marital status, educational qualifications, branch, medium, social status, native area, district, present stay, parental education, teaching parents, parental professions, monthly family income and type of family are given below.

Comparison across Sex

Table-1 indicates that there are significant differences between the comparison of male and female prospective teachers on their home and emotional adjustments. The results declared that both male and female prospective teachers' adjustment was good. In comparison it was observed that the female prospective teachers are adjusted better than males in home adjustment and males are adjusted better than females in emotional adjustment. There are no significant differences for the social, academic, health and total adjustments. The studies conducted by Lapsley et al (1987),Street and Kromrey (1994) and Lakshmi (1998) were consistent with the present study.

Comparison across Age

Table-2 indicates that there are no significant differences between the comparison of below 25 yrs and above 25 yrs prospective teachers on their adjustments. The results declared that below 25 yrs and above 25 yrs prospective teachers' adjustments were good. In comparison across age the prospective teachers are not having the significant differences for the home, social, emotional, academic, health and total adjustments. The study conducted by Takahashi and Majima (1994) results were not coincided with this study. Stuart Marcia Ciscely (2002) study states that the relationship between age and psychological adjustment was consistent with the study but, the study conducted by Grant, Smith, Sinclar and Salts (1993) found that age at the time of parental divorce affected the student's adjustment.

Comparison across Marital Status

Table-3 indicates that there are no significant differences between the comparison of married and un-married prospective teachers on their adjustments. The results declared that both married and un-married prospective teachers' adjustments were good. In comparison across marital status the prospective teachers are not having the significant differences for the home, social, emotional, academic, health and total adjustments. Grant, Smith, Sinclar and Salts (1993) study was consistent with the present study.

Comparison across Educational Qualifications

Table-4 indicates that there are significant differences between the comparison of graduate and post-graduate prospective teachers on their home, social, academic and total adjustments. The results declared that both graduate and post-graduate prospective teachers' adjustment was good. In comparison it was observed that the graduate prospective teachers are adjusted better than post-graduates in home, social, academic and total adjustments. There are no significant differences for the emotional and health adjustments.

Comparison across Branch

Table-5 indicates that there are significant differences between the comparison of Biological sciences, Physical sciences, Commerce and Arts faculty prospective teachers on their health and total adjustments. The results declared that Biological sciences, Physical sciences, Commerce and Arts faculty prospective teachers' adjustments were good. In comparison it was observed that the Physical sciences prospective teachers are adjusted better than others in health and total adjustments. There are no significant differences for the home, social, emotional and academic adjustments. Rajan, Ashrafullah and Rajan (1988) and Mohan and Kaur (1991) studies support the present study results.

Comparison across Medium

Table-6 indicates that there are significant differences between the comparison of English and Telugu medium prospective teachers on their social, emotional, academic, health and total adjustments. The results declared that English and Telugu medium prospective teachers' adjustments were good. In comparison it was observed that the English medium prospective teachers are adjusted better than Telugu in emotional adjustments and Telugu medium students are adjusted better than English in social, academic, health and total adjustments. There is no significant difference for the home adjustment dimension. Kasinath (1991), Barrat and Huba (1994) and Douglas, Alan Andrew, Lees (2005) studies results are consistent with the present study results.

Comparison across Social Status

Table-7 indicates that there are significant differences between the comparison of OC, BC, SC and ST community prospective teachers on their home, social, academic and total adjustments. The results declared that OC, BC, SC and ST community prospective teachers' adjustments were good. In comparison it was observed that the OC prospective teachers are adjusted better than others in home and social adjustments and BC students are adjusted better than others in academic and total adjustments. There were no significant differences for the emotional and health adjustment dimensions. The studies conducted by Bajpai (1999) and Ponraj and Packiam (1993) also support the results of the present study.

Comparison across Native Area

Table-8 indicates that there are significant differences between the comparison rural, urban and agency area prospective teachers on their home, social, academic and total adjustments. The results declared that rural, urban and agency area prospective teachers' adjustments were good. In comparison it was observed that the rural prospective teachers are adjusted better than others in social adjustment and urban students are adjusted better than others in home, academic and total adjustments. There are no significant differences for the emotional and health adjustment dimensions. Sujatha, Gaonkar, Khadi and Katarki (1993) and Renuka and Anuradha (2004) results of their studies are consistent where as Kasinath (1990)study results are inconsistent with the present study.

Comparison across District

Table-9 indicates that there are significant differences between the comparison of Srikakulam, Vizianagaram and Visakhapatnam prospective teachers on their emotional adjustment. The results declared that Srikakulam, Vizianagaram and Visakhapatnam prospective teachers' adjustments were good. In comparison it was observed that the Visakhapatnam prospective teachers are adjusted better than others in emotional adjustment. There are no significant differences for the home, social, academic, health and total adjustments.

Comparison across Present Stay

Table-10 indicates that there are significant differences between the comparisons of home, room and hostel resident prospective teachers on their home and academic adjustments. The results declared that home, room and hostel resident prospective teachers' adjustments were good. In comparison it was observed that the home resident prospective teachers are adjusted better than others in home and academic adjustments. There are no significant differences for the social, emotional, health and total adjustments. Barthelemy and Fine (1995) and Betten Court, Charton, Eubanks and Kernahan (1999) results of their studies were support the present study and Floyd (1988) study was inconsistent with the results.

Comparison across Parental Education

Table-11 indicates that there are significant differences between the comparison of educated parents, one parent educated and un-educated parents of prospective teachers on their home adjustment. The results declared that educated parents, one parent educated and un-educated parents of prospective teachers' adjustments were good. In comparison it was observed that the prospective teachers of educated parents are adjusted better than others in home adjustment. There are no significant differences for the social, emotional, academic, health and total adjustments. Alexander and Packiam (1998) study support the present study results that Mother's education influences students' adjustment.

Comparison across Teaching Parents

Table-12 indicates that there are significant differences between the comparison of both parents are teachers, father teacher, mother teacher and other than teaching profession parents of prospective teachers on their home, social, academic, health and total adjustments. The results declared that both parents are teachers, father teacher, mother teacher and other than teaching profession parents of prospective teachers' adjustments were good. In comparison it was observed that the other profession parents of prospective teachers are adjusted better than others in home, social, academic, health and total adjustments. There is no significant difference for the emotional adjustment dimension.

Comparison across Parental Professions

Table-13 indicates that there are significant differences between the comparison of parents working in agriculture, private jobs, government jobs and business of prospective teachers on their social adjustment. The results declared that parents working in agriculture, private jobs, government jobs and business of prospective teachers' adjustments were good. In comparison it was observed that the agricultural parents of prospective teachers are adjusted better than others in social adjustment. There are no significant differences for the home, emotional, academic, health and total adjustments.

Comparison across Monthly Family Income

The prospective teachers with the monthly family income below Rs. 5000/- are considered as low economic group. Students whose monthly family income ranged between Rs. 5000/- to Rs. 10000/- and between Rs. 10000/- to Rs. 20000/- are belonged to middle class categories respectively. High economic students are those whose monthly family income exceeded above Rs. 20000/-.

Table-14 indicates that there are no significant differences between the comparisons of economical aspects of prospective teachers on their adjustments. The results declared that all income groups of prospective teachers' adjustments were good. There are no significant differences for the home, social, emotional, academic, health and total adjustments of different income groups. The studies of Mohan and Kaur (1991), Miya and Krishna (1996), Mishra and Singh (1998) and Nabi Ahmed and Abdul Raheem (2003) did not supported the present study.

Comparison across Type of Family

Table-15 indicates that there are significant differences between the comparison of nuclear and joint family prospective teachers on their social adjustment. The results declared that both nuclear and joint family prospective teachers' adjustments were good. In comparison it was observed that the nuclear family prospective teachers are adjusted better than joint family in social adjustment. There are no significant differences for the home, emotional, academic, health and total adjustments. Natasha Datta (2003) study was inconsistent with the present study results.

SECTION-II
INTERACTION EFFECTS

The prospective teachers include both boys and girls studying in the colleges of education. So the independent variable gender has taken as an important dimension and the gender interactions of individual variables on adjustment were discussed. The interaction analyses were performed to examine the influence of these factors on adjustment.

Age and Gender

Table-16 indicates that there are no significant differences between the interaction of age and gender of the prospective teachers was observed on their adjustments. The results declared that both age groups of male and female prospective teachers' adjustments were good. But there are no significant differences between the interaction of age and gender of the prospective teachers on the home, social, emotional, academic, health and total adjustments. Lecci, Okun and Karoly (1994) and Stuart Marcia Ciscely (2002) studies results were supported the present study.

Marital Status and Gender

Table-17 indicates that there are no significant differences between the interaction of marital status and gender of the prospective teachers that was observed on their adjustments. The results declared that both married and un-married groups of male and female prospective teachers' adjustments were good. But there was no significant differences between the interaction of marital status and gender of the prospective teachers on the home, social, emotional, academic, health and total adjustments. Grant, Smith, Sinclar and Salts (1993) study results supported the present study.

Educational Qualifications and Gender

Table-18 shows the interaction effects of educational qualifications and gender on adjustment factors. A significant influence of the interaction of education and gender of the prospective teachers has been observed with regard to their evaluation of the adjustment. The results declared that both graduate and post-graduate groups of male and female prospective teachers' adjustments were good. Significant influence was observed with regard to the home, social, academic and total adjustments. More specifically, it is observed that graduate females are adjusted better in home and academic adjustments whereas graduate males are adjusted better in social and total adjustments. There are no significant differences for the emotional and health adjustments.

Branch and Gender

Table-19 shows the interaction of branch and gender on adjustment factors. A significant influence of the interaction of branch and gender of the prospective teachers has been observed with regard to their adjustment. The results declared that the four subject specialization groups of male and female prospective teachers' adjustments were good. Significant differences were observed with regard to health and total adjustments. More specifically, it is observed that female physical sciences students are adjusted better in health and total adjustments. There are no significant differences for the home, social, emotional and academic adjustments. Mohan and Kaur (1991) study results were consistent with the present study.

Medium and Gender

Table-20 shows the interaction of medium of instruction and gender on adjustment factors. A significant influence of the interaction of medium of instruction and gender of the prospective teachers has been observed with regard to their adjustment. The results declared that the both English and Telugu medium groups of male and female prospective teachers' adjustments were good. Significant differences were observed with regard to social, emotional, academic, health and total adjustments. More specifically, it is observed that male English medium students are adjusted better in emotional adjustment. Male students of Telugu medium are adjusted better in emotional adjustment. Female students of Telugu medium are adjusted better in academic, health and total adjustments. There is no significant difference for the home adjustment.

Social Status and Gender

Table-21 shows the interaction of social status and gender on adjustment factors. A significant influence of the interaction of social status and gender of the prospective teachers has been observed with regard to their adjustment. The results declared that the four OC, BC, SC and ST communities of male and female prospective teachers' adjustments were good. Significant differences were observed with regard to home, social, academic and total adjustments. More specifically, it is observed that OC female students are adjusted better in home adjustment. BC male students are adjusted better in social and total adjustments. BC female students are adjusted better in academic adjustment. There are no significant differences for the emotional and health adjustments.

Native Area and Gender

Table-22 shows the interaction of native area and gender on adjustment factors. A significant influence of the interaction of native area and gender of the prospective teachers has been observed with regard to their adjustment. The results declared that the rural, urban and agency area male and female prospective teachers' adjustments were good. Significant differences were observed with regard to home, social, academic and total adjustments. More specifically, it is observed that rural male students are adjusted better in social and total adjustments. Urban female students are adjusted better in home and academic adjustments. There are no significant differences for the emotional and health adjustments.

District and Gender

Table-23 shows the interaction of district and gender on adjustment factors. A significant influence of the interaction of district and gender of the prospective teachers has been observed with regard to their adjustment. The results declared that the Srikakulam, Vizianagaram and Visakhapatnam districts male and female prospective teachers' adjustments were good. Significant differences were observed with regard to emotional adjustment. More specifically, it is observed that male students of Visakhapatnam district are adjusted better in emotional adjustment. There are no significant differences for the home, social, academic, health and total adjustments.

Present Stay and Gender

Table-24 shows the interaction of present stay and gender on adjustment factors. A significant influence of the interaction of present stay and gender of the prospective teachers has been observed with regard to their adjustment. The results declared that the home, room and hostel residents of male and female prospective teachers' adjustments were good. Significant differences were observed with regard to home and academic adjustments. More specifically, it is observed that female home resident students are adjusted better in home and academic adjustments. There are no significant differences for the social, emotional, health and total adjustments.

Parental Education and Gender

Table-25 shows the interaction of parental education and gender on adjustment factors. A significant influence of the interaction of parental education and gender of the prospective teachers has been observed with regard to their adjustment. The results declared that the parents are educated, one parent educated and un-educated parents of male and female prospective teachers' adjustments were good. Significant differences were observed with regard to home adjustment. More specifically, it is observed that female students of educated parents are adjusted better in home adjustment. There are no significant differences for the social, emotional, academic, health and total adjustments.

Teaching Parents and Gender

Table-26 shows the interaction of teaching parents and gender on adjustment factors. A significant influence of the interaction of teaching parents and gender of the prospective teachers has been observed with regard to their adjustment. The results declared that the parents are teachers, father teacher, mother teacher and other profession parents of male and female prospective teachers' adjustments were good. Significant differences were observed with regard to home, social, academic, health and total adjustments. More specifically, it is observed that female students' mothers in teaching profession are adjusted better in home and total adjustments. Male students' parents working in other professions are adjusted better in social and health adjustments. Female students' parents working in other professions are adjusted better in academic adjustment. There is no significant difference for emotional adjustment.

Parental Professions and Gender

Table-27 shows the interaction of parental professions and gender on adjustment factors. A significant influence of the interaction of parental professions and gender of the prospective teachers has been observed with regard to their adjustment. The results declared that the agricultural parents, parents working in private jobs, parents working in government jobs and business parents of male and female prospective teachers' adjustments were good. Significant differences were observed with regard to social adjustment. More specifically, it is observed that female students of business parents are adjusted better in social adjustments. There are no significant differences for the home, emotional, academic, health and total adjustments.

Monthly Family Income and Gender

Table-28 shows the interaction of monthly income of the family and gender on adjustment factors. A non-significant influence of the interaction of monthly family income and gender of the prospective teachers has been observed with regard to their adjustment. The results declared that the four economic status groups of male and female prospective teachers' adjustments were good. No significant differences were observed with regard to adjustments. More specifically, it is observed that there are no significant differences for the home, social, emotional, academic, health and total adjustments. Mohan and Kaur (1991) study results were inconsistent with the present study.

Type of Family and Gender

Table-29 shows the interaction of type of family and gender on adjustment factors. A significant influence of the interaction of type of family and gender of the prospective teachers has been observed with regard to their adjustment. The results declared that the nuclear and joint families of male and female prospective teachers' adjustments were good. Significant differences were observed with regard to social adjustment. More specifically, it is observed that male students of nuclear families are adjusted better in social adjustment. There are no significant differences for the home, emotional, academic, health and total adjustments.

SECTION-III
CORRELATION ANALYSIS

This section includes the discussion regarding the relationship between the home adjustment, social adjustment, emotional adjustment, academic adjustment, health adjustment and total adjustment dimensions.

Inter Correlation Matrix of Adjustment

The home adjustment dimension in relationship with other dimensions like social adjustment, emotional adjustment, academic adjustment, health adjustment and total adjustments are statistically significant and positively correlated. The home adjustment dimension measures the degree of adjustment in relationship with the degree of adjustment of other dimensions. The results indicated that the better home adjustment leads to better social, emotional, academic, health and total adjustments.

The social adjustment dimension in relationship with other dimensions like home adjustment, emotional adjustment, academic adjustment, health adjustment and total adjustments are statistically significant and positively correlated. The social adjustment dimension measures the degree of adjustment in relationship with the degree of adjustment of other dimensions. The results indicated that the better social adjustment leads to better home, emotional, academic, health and total adjustments.

The emotional adjustment dimension in relationship with other dimensions like home adjustment, social adjustment, academic adjustment, health adjustment and total adjustments are statistically significant and positively correlated. The emotional adjustment dimension measures the degree of adjustment in relationship with the degree of adjustment of other dimensions. The results indicated that the better emotional adjustment leads to better home, social, academic, health and total adjustments. Gerdes and Mallickrodt (1994) study results coincide with the present study.

The academic adjustment dimension in relationship with other dimensions like home adjustment, social adjustment, emotional adjustment, health adjustment and total adjustments are statistically significant and positively correlated. The academic adjustment dimension measures the degree of adjustment in relationship with the degree of adjustment of other dimensions. The results indicated that the better academic adjustment leads to better home, social, emotional, health and total adjustments.

The health adjustment dimension in relationship with other dimensions like home adjustment, social adjustment, emotional adjustment, academic adjustment and total adjustments are statistically significant and positively correlated. The health adjustment dimension measures the degree of adjustment in relationship with the degree of adjustment of other dimensions. The results indicated that the better health adjustment leads to better home, social, emotional, academic and total adjustments.

The total adjustment dimension in relationship with other dimensions like home adjustment, social adjustment, emotional adjustment, academic adjustment and health adjustments are statistically significant and positively correlated. The total adjustment dimension measures the totalities of home, social, emotional, academic and health adjustment dimensions.

Summary

The adjustment dimensions were measuring their respective quality. Verbally they are different whereas in social situations; the dimensions collectively measure the adjustments. It means there is an overlapping of other dimensions done for measuring a single dimension.

Adjustment is a collective behaviour so the dimensions collectively measure the degree of adjustment. The psychological, sociological, environmental factors intermingled with the life situations in a college. So the distinguish variations were collectively measured.

The study 'adjustment of prospective teachers' was conducted based on the dimensions of adjustment related to psychological, sociological and environmental aspects. The comparisons related to adjustment dimensions on individual dimensions were made in this study.

This chapter focused on comparisons of the adjustment factors across the individual factors are discussed in an organized and systematic way. From the significant results and their discussion, certain conclusions were drawn and presented in the next chapter.

CHAPTER 6 Summary and Conclusions

In India the majority of people live in villages, mandals and small towns. The students, who want to study teacher education from the rural areas, will have to get admission into colleges of education located at mandals or district head quarters or university campuses.

The prospective teachers have to face new environmental situations in the colleges of education located in other places. The prospective teachers of all academic courses constitute a group of heterogeneity and complexity which is due to the variations prevalent among them in terms of region, locality, custom, language, style, caste, religion etc. In this complex situation the only way is to adjust to the environmental situations.

In the process of adjustment, the prospective teachers have to face two types of adjustments. One type of adjustment is related to self or personality factors to adjust and the other adjustment is related to the environmental factors or situational factors to adjust in the college of education and the prospective teacher living society.

The adjustment is an older concept meaning the degree of harmonious relationship between the individual and the varying situations in the colleges of education. The better adjustments lead to better academic achievement, better personal / emotional adjustment and better group relations in the college of education or in the resident society.

The present study is intended to conduct along with these lines with adjustment factors in comparison across the different individual variables. The observations on these lines will make to select some related studies.

A review of literature on selected variables has been carried out and it has been observed the adjustment factors on students. Overall the studies indicated that the personality factors as well as environmental factors influence the adjustment of the students. Most of the studies concluded that better personality factors lead to better environmental adjustment of the students.

The present study is measuring the adjustment factors of prospective teachers studying in colleges of education and it was focused on the comparisons related to different independent variables. The major objectives of the study are: 1) To examine the adjustment of prospective teachers and the impact of individual factors on their adjustment, 2) To examine the impact of gender interactions of individual variables on adjustments and 3) To examine the relationship between adjustment variables.

The hypotheses framed for the study to test are: 1) Individual variables will have a significant influence on adjustment. 2) The interactions of individual variables will have a significant influence on adjustment. 3) Adjustment variables are expected to have a significant relationship between them.

The independent variables of the present study are sex, age, marital status, educational qualifications, branch, medium, social status, native area, district, present stay, parental education, teaching parents, parental professions, monthly family income and type of family. The dependent variables are home, social, emotional, academic, health and total adjustments.

Two standardized questionnaires were used to measure the above factors. They are 1) The adjustment inventory, constructed by Srivastava and Govind Tiwari (1986) and 2) The Indian adaptation of Bell's adjustment inventory, constructed by Lalita Sharma (1988).The two questionnaires were published by Agra Psychological Research Cell, Tiwari Kothi, Belanganj, Agra, India.

The final study was conducted on a sample of 1400 prospective teachers studying B.Ed course in colleges of education situated in North Coastal Andhra, affiliated to Andhra University, Visakhapatnam. The North Coastal Andhra is expanded to the three districts of Srikakulam, Vizianagaram and Visakhapatnam.

The data were collected from the colleges of education of the above three districts. The samples of respondents have been categorized according to the individual factors. The data were analyzed by using t-tests, One-way analysis of variance tests, Multivariate analysis tests and Pearson's product moment coefficient of correlations.

The following findings are drawn from the analysis of the data.

Findings of the Study

- Female students are better in home adjustment and males are better in emotional adjustment.
- There was no significant difference of age factor on the adjustment of prospective teachers.
- There was no significant difference of marital status on the adjustment of prospective teachers.
- Graduate prospective teachers are adjusted better than post-graduate prospective teachers in home, social, academic and total adjustments.
- Prospective teachers of Physical sciences and Arts faculties are adjusted better in health and total adjustments.
- Prospective teachers of Telugu medium are adjusted better in social, academic, health and total adjustments and English medium are adjusted better in emotional adjustment.

- Prospective teachers of OC are adjusted better in home, social and BC are in academic and total adjustments.
- Urban prospective teachers are adjusted better in home, academic and total adjustments and rural prospective teachers are adjusted better in social adjustment.
- Visakhapatnam district prospective teachers are adjusted better in emotional adjustment.
- Home resident prospective teachers are adjusted better in home and academic adjustments.
- Prospective teachers of educated parents are adjusted better in home adjustment.
- Prospective teachers' parents working other than teacher jobs are adjusted better in home, social, academic, health and total adjustments.
- Prospective teachers' parents working in agriculture are adjusted better in social adjustment.
- There was no significant difference of monthly family income on the adjustment of prospective teachers.
- Prospective teachers from nuclear families are adjusted better in social adjustment.
- There was no significant difference between the interaction of age and gender of the prospective teachers on adjustment.
- There was no significant difference between the interaction of marital status and gender of the prospective teachers on adjustment.
- Graduate females are adjusted better in home and academic adjustments whereas graduate males are adjusted better in social and total adjustments.
- Female physical sciences students are adjusted better in health and total adjustments.
- Male English medium students are adjusted better in emotional adjustment. Male students of Telugu

medium are adjusted better in emotional adjustment. Female students of Telugu medium are adjusted better in academic, health and total adjustments.

- OC female students are adjusted better in home adjustment. BC male students are adjusted better in social and total adjustments. BC female students are adjusted better in academic adjustment.
- Rural male students are adjusted better in social and total adjustments. Urban female students are adjusted better in home and academic adjustments.
- Male students of Visakhapatnam district are adjusted better in emotional adjustment.
- Female home resident students are adjusted better in home and academic adjustments.
- Female students of educated parents are adjusted better in home adjustment.
- Female students' mothers in teaching profession are adjusted better in home and total adjustments. Male students' parents working in other professions are adjusted better in social and health adjustments. Female students' parents working in other professions are adjusted better in academic adjustment.
- Female students of business parents are adjusted better in social adjustments.
- There was no significant difference between the interaction of monthly family income and gender of the prospective teachers on adjustment.
- Male students of nuclear families are adjusted better in social adjustment.
- The inter correlations between the adjustment dimensions are all positively correlated. This indicates that the better adjustment in one dimension leads to better adjustment in other dimension.

The results and findings presented above are generalized in the present study. Firstly the adjustment dimensions are generalized in the comparisons across different individual factors of the prospective teachers. Secondly, the adjustment dimensions generalized in comparison across gender interactions of different individual factors of the prospective teachers. Finally, the relationships between the variables related to adjustments are generalized.

In the light of the above findings, certain conclusions can be drawn regarding the adjustment of prospective teachers.

Conclusions of the Study

- Gender differences were observed between male and female prospective teachers in the dimensions of home and emotional adjustments.
- The age factor has no influence on the adjustment of prospective teachers.
- Marital status has no influence on the adjustment of prospective teachers.
- Educational qualifications have influence over the dimensions of home, social, academic and total adjustment dimensions of graduate and post-graduate prospective teachers.
- The variable 'branch' has an influence on the health and total adjustments of prospective teachers with different subject specializations.
- The variable 'medium' has an influence on the dimensions of social, emotional, academic, health and total adjustment of prospective teachers.
- The social status of the prospective teachers has an influence on the dimensions of home, social, academic and total adjustment dimensions.
- The native area of the prospective teachers has an influence on the dimensions of home, social, academic and total adjustments.
- The variable 'district' has an influence on the emotional adjustment of prospective teachers.

- The variable 'present stay' of the prospective teachers has an influence on the home and academic adjustment dimensions.
- The education of the parents has an influence on the home adjustment of the prospective teachers.
- The variable 'teaching parents' has an influence on the home, social, academic, health and total adjustment dimensions of prospective teachers.
- The parental professions influences the social adjustment of prospective teachers.
- The monthly family income has no influence on the adjustment of prospective teachers.
- The variable 'type of family' has an influence on the social adjustment of prospective teachers.

Apart from the above conclusions, certain recommendations may be made for the prospective teachers studying in colleges of education in North Coastal Andhra.

Recommendations of the Study

- The prospective teachers may be provided with a more conducive atmosphere to study and proper training to bring out the best from them.
- The prospective teachers who are suffering from psychological problems are recommended to take psychological help from the counsellor or psychologist or mentor.
- Related to the health adjustment of prospective teachers, physical exercises, aerobics, the relaxation techniques, yoga and meditation are recommended.
- The negative emotions can be eliminated by spiritual adjustment, coping strategies, aesthetic adjustments and development of positive thinking.
- Good and friendly relationships should be maintained among the prospective teachers with co-operation and help to others in the colleges of education.

- Good social relationships should be maintained in the living environment when the prospective teachers are engaged in project work, teaching practice or any out side work.
- Rural background prospective teachers need communication skills training, technical skills and computer skill training.
- The DSC preparation is needed from the beginning of the course. Prospective teachers are recommended to work hard because it is a competitive world.
- The vocational counselling is recommended for prospective teachers to choose better placements after the completion of their B.Ed programme.

Suggestions for Further Research

Future research can be conducted on the basis of some of the findings obtained in the present study.

It may be worth while to include a few personality variables like teaching aptitude, patience, level of aspiration, communication skills, technical ability, leadership, language ability, moral values, class room management, personality development, professional interest and dedication, logical thinking, sense of humor, personal authority etc.

It may be useful to include a few adjustment variables like infrastructure, institution facilities, teaching and non-teaching staff, curricular and co-curricular activities, project work, writing of records, practical work, social service like clean and green, NGC (National green corps), literacy programmes, rules of discipline and attendance, library usage, internship and intensive teaching practice, cultural programmes and functions etc.

It may be worthwhile to include a few individual factors like caste, religion, region, customs and traditions, parent child relationships, parent-teacher associations, peer group relationships, family relationships, cross cultural variations, smoking behaviour, alcohol and drug use etc.

The comparisons across different districts prospective teachers within the state, the comparisons across different university prospective teachers in the state and country and the comparisons across different university prospective teachers in different nations can be done to examine the differences in adjustment of prospective teachers.

Bibliography

Abe, J., Talbot, D.M., & Geelhoed, R.J. (1998). Effects of a peer programme on International student adjustment. *Journal of College Student Development, **36(9)***, 539-547.

Adan, A.M., & Felner, R.D. (1995). Ecological Congruence and adaptation of minority youth during the transition to college. *Journal of Community Psychology, **23(3)***, 256-269.

Adler, A. (1930). *The Science of Living*. New York: Allen and Unwin.

Alexander, E.J., & Packiam, S. (1998). The adjustment problems of rural and urban school going adolescents. *The progress of Education, **5***, 107-110.

Alford, Linda, J. (2007).Impact of inter parental conflict on adjustment of African, American college students from divorced and intact families. *Dissertation Abstract International, **68(4)**,* 1534.

Allport, G.W. (1961). *Pattern and Growth in personality,* New York: Holt, Rinehard and Winston.

Aspinwall, L.G., & Taylor, S.E. (1992). Modeling cognitive adaptation: A longitudinal investigation of the impact of individual differences and coping on college adjustment and performance. *Journal of Personality and Social Psychology, **63(6)***, 989-1003.

Bajpai, S. (1999). Effects of Caste belongingness on Adjustment of high school girls. *The progress of Education, **12***, 274-277.

Balaisis, Mary (2004). 1st year students' adjustment at Vilnius University in Lithuania: The role of self-orientation, locus of control, social support and demographic variables. *Dissertation Abstract International, **65(10)**,* 3687.

Barratt, M.F., & Huba, M.E. (1994). Factors related to International undergraduate student adjustment in an American Community. *College Student Journal, **28(4)**,* 422-436.

Barthelemy, K.J., & Fine, M. A. (1995). The relations between residence hall climate and adjustment in college students. *College Student Journal, **29(4)**,* 465-475.

Bell, H.M. (1962). *Manuel, Bell adjustment Inventory* (Revised Student form, P:3). California.

Bettencourt, B. A., Chartton, K., Eubanks, J., & Kernahan, C. (1999). Development of Collective self-esteem among students: predicting adjustment to college. *Basis & Applied Social Psychology, **21(3)**,* 213-222.

Bernard, L.C., Hutchison, S., Lavin, A., & Pennington, P. (1996). Ego-strength, Hardiness, self-esteem, self-efficacy, optimism and maladjustment: Health - related personality constructs and the "Big five" model of personality. *Assessment, **3(2)**,* 115-131.

Berndt, T. J., Miller, K.E., & Park, K. (1989). Adolescents' perceptions of friends' and parents' influence on aspects of their school adjustment. *Journal of Early Adolescence, **9(4)**,* 419-435.

Bhaskar Rao, D. & Harshitha, D. (2004). *Adjustment of Adolescents*. New Delhi: Discovery publishing House.

Bhatia, H.R. (1965). *Elements of Social Psychology.* Bombay, India: Manaktalas.

Bhatnagar, R.P. (1968). A study of some of the personality factors as predictors of academic achievement. *C.I.E. Studies in Education and Psychology*, (P.63). New Delhi: National Council of Educational Research and Training.

Boring (1948). *Foundations of Psychology,* New York: John Wiley & sons Inc.

Bridges, K.R. (1991, June). Psychology of adjustment at Research Universities. *Psychological Reports, **68(pt2)**,* 1130.

Brooks, J.H., & DuBois, D. L. (1995). Individual and environmental predictors of adjustment during the first year of College. *Journal of the College Student Development, **36(4)**,* 347-360.

Buch, M.B. (Ed.) (1991). *Survey of Research in Education*, New Delhi: NCERT.

Campbell, Donald Bruce (2002). Caribbean students' adjustment to a culture at a small liberal arts college. *Dissertation Abstract International* ,***63(6)***, 2154.

Carlisle-Frank, P.L. (1992). The relocation experience: Analysis of factors thought to influence adjustment to transition. *Psychological Reports*, ***70(3, pt 1)***, 835-838.

Carter, Elizabeth (2006). Parental assistance and 1st year college students' independence and Adjustment. *Dissertation Abstract International* ***67(11)***, 4348.

Chartrand, J. M. (1990). A causal analysis to predict the personal and academic adjustment of non-traditional students. *Journal of Counselling Psychology*, ***37(1)***, 65-73.

Chartrand, J. M. (1992). An empirical test of a model of non-traditional student adjustment. *Journal of Counselling Psychology*, ***39(2)***, 193-202.

Chaudhary, B.K., & Sinha, R. B. (1992). A study of adjustment in relation to some personality factors. *Indian Journal of Psychometry & Education*, ***23(1)***, 33-36b.

Chaudhury, P.R., & Basu, J. (1998). Parent-child relationship school achievement and adjustment of adolescent boys. *Journal of Community Guidance and Research*, ***15(2)***, 215-266.

Chauhan, S.S. (1979). *Advanced Educational Psychology*, New Delhi: Vikas Publishing House Pvt., Ltd.

Cherian, V.I., & Cherian. L. (1998). University students' adjustment problems. *Psychological Reports*, ***82(3 pt 2)***, 1135-1138.

Chiu, M. L. (1995). The influence of anticipatory fear on foreign student adjustment: An exploratory study. *International Journal of Intercultural relations*, ***19(1)***, 1-44.

Clinton, A. M., & Anderson, L. R. (1999). Social and emotional loneliness: Gender differences and relationships with self-monitoring and perceived control. *Journal of Black Psychology*, ***25(1)***, 61-77.

Coe, W.C. (1972). *Challenges of personal adjustment*. San Francisco: Rinehart Press.

Coleman, J.C. (1969). *Abnormal psychology and modern life* (3rd Ed.). Bombay, India: Taraporevala, D.B. and Co., (P). Ltd.

Crow, L.D, & Alice Crow (1956).*Understanding our Behavior*, New York: Alfred A. Knoff.

Damji, T., Clement, R., & Noels, K. A. (1996). Acculturation mode, identity variation and psychosocial adjustment. *Journal of Social Psychology, **136(4)***, 493-500.

Dandekar, W.N. (1981). *Psychological foundations of Education,* Madras, India: McMillan India Limited.

Debbie Chiodo, David A. Wolfe, Claire Crooks, Ray Hughes & Pete Jaffe (2009).Impact of sexual harassment Victimization by Peers on subsequent adolescent Victimization an adjustment: A longitudinal study- *Online publication.*

Defour, D.C., & Hirsch, B.J. (1990). The adaptation of Black graduate students: A social network approach. *American Journal of Community Psychology, **18(3)***, 487-503.

Dewall, Deborah Ann Baker (2005). Family relationship and college adjustment of first generation college students. *Dissertation Abstract International, **66(4)***, 1290.

Douglas, Alan Andrew, Lees (2005). Still in transition: An ethnographic case study of the academic and cultural adjustment experiences of Kuwaiti students enrolled in a formal agreement partnership between an American University and the state of Kuwait. *Dissertation Abstract International, **66(4)***, 1290.

Drever, James (1952).*A Dictionary of Psychology*, Middlesex: Penguin Books, p-10.

Duckworth, Linda wing (2002). International students' leadership involvement and cross-cultural adjustment: Two case students. *Dissertation Abstract International, **63(3)***, 874.

Essau, C.A., & Trommsdorff, G. (1996). Coping with University - related problems: A Cross Cultural Comparison. *Journal of Cross-Cultural Psychology, **27(3)**,* 315-328.

Eysenck, H.J. (1978). *The structure of Human Personality.* London: Methuen and Co., Ltd.

Eysenck, H.J., & Eysenck, S.B.G. (1975). *Manual of the Eysenck personality Inventory.* San Diego: Educational and Industrial testing services.

Floyd, N.E. (1988). Family experience and college residential adjustment: Case examples from an experimental living-learning programme. *College Student Journal,* ***22(4),*** 342-348.

Fox, Daniel Paul (2000). Interactive effects of gender, ethnicity and first year experience program participation on college student adjustment, *Dissertation Abstract International,* ***61(8),*** 3007.

Furukawa, T. (1997). Cultural distance and its relationship to psychological adjustment of International exchange students. *Psychiatry and Clinical. Neuroscience,* ***51(3),*** 87-91.

Furukawa, T., & Shibayama, T. (1993). Predicting maladjustment of exchange students in different cultures: A prospective study. *Social Psychiatry and Psychiatrical Epidemiology,* ***28(3),*** 142-146.

Gajdzik, patrycia, K. (2006). Relationship between self-efficacy beliefs and socio-cultural adjustment of international graduate students and American graduate students. *Dissertation Abstract International,* ***66 (10),*** 3564.

Garbarino, C., & Strange, C. (1993). College adjustment and family environments of students reporting parental alcohol problems. *Journal of College Student Development,* ***34(4),*** 261-266.

Gates, A.S., & Jersild, A.T. (1973). *Educational Psychology,* (p: 614-615), New York: McMillan and Co.

Gerdes, H., & Mallinckrodt, B. (1994). Emotional, Social and Academic adjustment of college students: A longitudinal study of retention. *Journal of Counselling & Development,* ***72(3),*** 281-288.

Getzels, J.W., (1975). "A social psychology of Education", in Lindzey, G., & Aronson, E (Ed), *The handbook of social psychology,* (2nd Edition, Vol. V). New Delhi: Amerind Publishing Company Pvt., Ltd.

Good, C.V. (1945). *Dictionary of Education,* (p: 6). New York: McGraw Hill Book Co., Inc.

Gorlow, K. (1968). *Readings in the psychology of Adjustment.* New York: Mc Graw-Hill Book Company.

Grant, L.S., Smith, T. A., Sinclair, J. J., & Salts, C. J. (1993). The impact of parental divorce on college adjustment. *Journal of Divorce and Remarriage,* ***19(1-2),*** 183-193.

Graziano, W. G., Jensen - Campbell, L. A., & Finch. J. F. (1997). The self as a mediator between personality and adjustment. *Journal of Personality and Social Psychology,* ***73(2),*** 392-404.

Greenier, K.D., Kernis, M.H., McNamara, C.W., & Waschull, S.B. (1999). Individual differences in reactivity to daily events: Examining the roles of stability and level of self-esteem. *Journal of Personality,* ***67(1),*** 185-208.

Hadley, Wanda (2002). The adjustment to the academic expectations at a private, four year selective university of traditional age, 1st year residential students with specific learning disabilities . *Dissertation Abstract International,* ***63(1),*** 108.

Haemmerlie, F.M., Steen, S.C., & Benedicto. J. A. (1994). Undergraduates' conflictual independence, adjustment and alcohol use: The importance of the mother - student relationship. *Journal of Clinical Psychology,* ***50(4),*** 644-650.

Halamandaris, K. F., & Power, K.G. (1997). Individual differences, dysfunctional attitudes and social support: A study of the psychosocial adjustment to University life of home students. *Personality and Individual differences,* ***1(22),*** 93-104.

Hall, C.S., & Lindzey, G. (1978). *Theories of Personality* (3rd Ed.). New York: John Wiley & Sons.

Heather, J. Smith (2009).Every day interactions with university authorities: Authority treatment quality, outcome favourability and first year students' university adjustment. *Group processes & Inter group relations,* ***12(2),*** 209-226.

Henning, K., Ey, S., & Shaw, D. (1998). Perfectionism, the imposter phenomenon and psychological adjustment in Medical, Dental, Nursing and Pharmacy students. *Medical Education,* ***32(5),*** 456-464.

Hill, Celeste Harris (2005). Adjustment among college students experiencing parental divorce as young adults. *Dissertation Abstract International,* ***67 (4),*** 1222.

Hinkle, Sara. E. (2005).Making the transition: The adjustment experiences of first year students attending a pre-college academic programme. *Dissertation Abstract International, **65(11)***, 4127.

Holmbeck, G. N., & Wandrei, M. L. (1993). Individual and relational predictors of adjustment in first-year college students. *Journal of Counseling Psychology,* ***40(1),*** 73-78.

Howie, Jessica Danielle (2004). The influence of friendship group ethnicity on the college adjustment of African-American students: A comparison of students at a predominantly white and at a diverse institution. *Dissertation Abstract International, 65 (II)*, 4102.

Hussain, S., & Kumari, M. (1995). Eysenck's personality dimensions in relation to ego-strength and adjustment. *Journal of personality & Clinical studies,* ***11 (1-2),*** 43-48.

Ichiyama, M. A., Colbert, D., Laramore, H., & Heim, M. (1993). Self-concealment and correlates of adjustment in college students. *Journal of College Student Psychotherapy,* ***7(4),*** 55-68.

Iwata, O. (1994). The relationships of intolerance for waiting - stress with health and personality, 25th international congress of psychology (1992, Brussels, Belgium). *Psychologia: An international Journal of Psychology in the Orient,* ***37(2),*** 81-88.

Jay, G.M., & D' Augelli, A. R. (1991). Social support and adjustment to University life: A comparison of African - American and White freshmen. *Journal of Community Psychology,* ***19(2),*** 95-108.

Jou, Y. H., & Fukada, H. (1995). Effect of social support from various sources on the adjustment of Chinese students in Japan. *Journal of Social Psychology,* ***135(3),*** 305-311.

Jou, Y.H., & Fukada, H. (1996a). Cross-cultural adjustment of Chinese students in Japan. *Psychological Reports,* ***78(2),*** 435-444.

Jou, Y.H., & Fukada, H. (1996b). Influence of social supports and personality on adjustment of Chinese students in Japan. *Journal of applied social psychology,* ***26(20),*** 1795-1802.

Kaczmarek, P.G., Matlock, G, Merta, R, & Ames, M.H. (1994). An Assessment of International College student's adjustment. *International Journal for the advancement of Conselling,* ***17(4),*** 241-247.

Kasinath, H.M. (1991). Adjustment between migrated Hindi and non-Hindi speaking students studying in Jawahar Navodaya Vidyalayas. *The Progress of Education,* ***9,*** 8-10.

Kasinath, M.M. (1990). Adjustment in Navodaya Vidyalayas. *The Progress of Education,* ***1,*** 8-11.

Kelly, Warren, L. (2006).Psychological adjustment, behaviour and health problems in multi racial young adults. *Dissertation Abstract International ,* ***67(11),*** 4347.

Kenny, M. E., & Donaldson, G. A. (1992). The relationship of Parental attachment of First year College Women. *Journal of College Student Development,* ***33 (5),*** 431-438.

Kenny, M. E., & Rice. K.G. (1995). Attachment to parents and adjustment in late adolescent college students: Current status, applications, and future considerations. *Counselling psychologist,* ***23(3),*** 433-456.

Kenrick, D.T., McCreath, H.E., Govern, J., & King, R. (1990). Person environment intersections: Everyday settings and Common trait dimensions. *Journal of Personality & Social Psychology,* ***58(4),*** 685-698.

Khan, R. (1991). Study of adjustment in relation to some personality and personal background factors among college students. *Indian Psychological Review,* ***36(1-2),*** 38-39.

Kiefer, Sarah, M., & Ryan, Allison, M. (2008).Striving for social dominance over peers. The implications for academic adjustment during early adolescence. *Journal of Educational Psychology,* ***100(2),*** 417-428.

Krishnan, K., & Sundaram. A.M. (1992). Hostel Adjustment Inventory. *The Educational Review,* ***11,*** 181-185.

Kulshrestha, S.P. (1979). *Educational Psychology.* Meerut, India: Loyal Book Depot.

Lakshmi, V. (1998). Adjustment of androgynous persons. *Praachi Journal of Psycho-cultural dimensions,* ***14(2),*** 149-152.

Lalita Sharma (1988).*Indian Adaptation of Bell's Adjustment Inventory*, Agra psychological Research Cell, Tiwari Kothi, Belanganj, Agra.

Lapsley, D.K., Rice, K.G., & Fitz Gerald, D.P. (1990). Adolescent attachment identity and adjustment to college: Implications for the continuity of adaptation hypothesis. *Journal of Counselling & Development,* ***68(5)*****,** 561-565.

Lapsley, D.K., Rice, K.G., & Shadid, G.E. (1989). Psychological separation and adjustment to college. *Journal of Counselling Psychology,* ***36(3)*****,** 286-294.

Lazarus, R.S. (1976). *Patterns of adjustment.* Tokyo, Japan: McGraw-Hill, Kogakusha Pvt.Ltd.

Lecci, L., Okun, M. A., & Karoly, P. (1994). Life regrets and current goals as predictors of psychological adjustment. *Journal of Personality & Social Psychology,* ***66(4)*****,** 731-741.

Leong, F.T.L., Bonz, M.H., & Zachar, P. (1997). Coping styles as predictors of college adjustment among freshmen. *Counselling Psychology Quarterly*, ***10(2)*****,** 211-220.

Leong, F. T., Mallinckrodt, B., & Kralj, M. M. (1990). Cross-cultural variations in stress and adjustment among Asian and Caucasian graduate students. *Journal of Multicultural Counselling & Development*, ***18(1)*****,** 19-28.

Lindgren, H.C. (1959). *Psychology of personal and social adjustment* (2nd Ed). New York: American Book Company.

Lindgren, Beth Maxine (2003).An Assessment of academic experiences formal and informal out of classroom experiences, and overall adjustment of freshman students at a mid western public four-year institution compared to students at other public universities. *Dissertation Abstract International,* ***64(8)****,* 2805.

Lopez, F. G. (1991). Patterns of family conflict and their relation to college student adjustment. *Journal of Counselling & Development,* ***69(3)***, 257-260.

Mangal, S.K. (1989). *Advanced Educational psychology.* New Delhi: Eastern Economy Edition, Prentice Hall Incorporation, p-393&394.

Margaret L. Kern & Howard S. Fried Man (2009).Early educational milestones as predictors of life long academic achievement, middle life achievement and longevity. *University of California, Reverside, USA-Online publication.*

Marie Vafors Fritz, Dorothy Chin & Valirie De Marinis (2008).Stressors, Anxiety, acculturation and adjustment among International and North American students-*Online publication.*

Martin, N.K., & Dixon, P.N. (1989). The effects of freshman orientation and locus of control on adjustment to college. *Journal of College Student Development, **30(4)***, 362-367.

Martin, N. K., & Dixon, P. N. (1994). The effects of freshman orientation and locus of control on adjustment to college: A Follow-up study. *Social behaviour & personality, **22(2)***, 201-208.

Mishra, S., & Singh, R.D. (1998). Personality adjustment of graduates with reference to their socioeconomic status. *Praachi Journal of Psycho-cultural dimensions, **14(1)***, 43-44.

Mitra, S.K., & Bhatkal, R.G. (Eds.). (1972). *A Survey of Research in Psychology*: A project sponsored by The Indian Council of Social Science Research, New Delhi. Bombay, India: Popular Prakashan.

Miya, I., & Krishna, K.P. (1996). Adjustment problem among socio-economically deprived adolescents. *Indian Journal of Psychological Issues, **4(1)***, 32-35.

Mohan, J., & Kaur, M. (1991). A study of adjustment of University Research Scholars in relation to their values and socio-economic status. *Indian psychological Review, **36(5-6)***, 9-18.

Monroe, P. (Ed.) (1990). *International Encyclopedia of Education.* New Delhi: Cosmo publications.

Montgomery, R.L., & Haemmerlie, F. M. (1993). Undergraduate adjustment to College, drinking behaviour and fraternity membership. *Psychological Reports, **73(3, pt 1)***, 801-802.

Mooney, S. P., Sherman, M.F., & Lopresto, C. T. (1991). Academic locus of control self esteem and perceived distance from home as predictors of college adjustment. *Journal of Counselling & Development, **69(5)***, 445-448.

Morgan, Valerie Ann (2005). Outdoor experimental team-building and the college adjustment and persistence of freshmen in learning communities. *Dissertation Abstract International, **67 (2)**,* 486.

Mukhopadyay, P., De. S., Chattopadhyay. K., & Biswas, D. (1996). "Deprivation": its impact on arousal modulation and adjustment. A psycho-physiological approach. *Indian Journal of Clinical psychology, **23(2)***, 161-169.

Nabi Ahmed & Abdul Raheem (2003). Intelligence, Socio Economic Status and adjustment as correlates of academic achievement. *The Educational Review*, ***46(9)***, 6-9.

Natasha Datta (2003).The relationship of family environment and academic performance to college adjustment of 1st generation, low income college students after a summer program and fall semester transition. *Dissertation Abstract International* , ***63(12)***, 4222-A.

Nelson, W. L., Hughes, H.M., Handal, P., & Katz, B. (1993). The relationship of family structure and family conflict to adjustment in young adult college students. *Adolescence*, ***28(109)***, 29-40.

O'Connell, V., & O' Connell, A. (1974). *Choice and change: An Introduction to psychology of growth.* New Jersey: Prentice – Hall, Inc.Engle Wood Cliffs.

Odera, P., & Hasan, Q. (1995). Problems of adjustment to a foreign culture. *Journal of Community Guidance and Research*, ***12(1)***, 63-75.

Oravecz, Joseph (2002). The use of outdoors experiential education in higher education: An investigation of factors in wilderness orientation programmes that influence student adjustment. *Dissertation Abstract International*, ***63 (5)***, 1743.

Patricia, Gale Harrist (2006).1st year students' adjustment to a university: the role of e-mentoring. *Dissertation Abstract International*, ***67(11)***, 4103.

Pettus, Karen Rosenbalm (2006).The relationships of parental monitoring to community college student adjustment and achievement: Differences by gender ethnicity, parental education level and student residence. *Dissertation Abstract International*, ***67(7)***, 2465.

Pennebaker, J.W., Colder, M., & Sharp, L.K. (1990). Accelerating the coping process. *Journal of personality and social psychology*, ***58(3)***, 528-537.

Pfeil, lynn Rigle (2000). Parental attachment, attachment style and college adjustment in African American students, *Dissertation Abstract International* , ***61(10)***, 3892A.

Ponraj, J.P., & Packiam, S. (1993). Adjustment problems of adolescents. *The progress of Education*, **2,** 42-45.

Prasad, R.S. (1993). A study of adjustment in relation to social integration and achievement of the students of Residential schools, Waltair. *Unpublished Ph.D., Thesis,* Andhra University, Visakhapatnam: India.

Protinsky, H., & Gilkey, J.K. (1996). An empirical investigation of the construct of personality authority in late adolescent women and their level of college adjustment. *Adolescence,* ***31(122),*** 291-295.

Rajan, S.S., Ashrafullah, A.M., & Rajan, V.N. (1988). Adjustment problems of professional and non-professional college students. *The progress of Education,* **3,** 56-59.

Ramanaiah, N.V., Byravan, A., & ThuHien, N. (1996). Weinberger adjustment typology and the five-factor model of personality. *Psychological Reports,* ***78(2),*** 432-434.

Rao, V., & Yadav, S. (1992). Adjustment problems of adolescent girls in relation to family size and birth order. *Journal of Community Guidance and Research,* ***9(1)***, 51-57.

Ray, A. (1992). Personality adjustment and academic achievement. *Psychological Research Journal,* ***16(2),*** 43-51.

Reggio, R.E., Watring, K.P., & Throckmorton, B. (1993). Social skills, social support and psychosocial adjustment. *Personality and Individual differences,* ***15(3)***, 275-280.

Rehulkova, O., Blatny, M., & Osecka, L. (1995). Adolescents coping styles: A relation to the temperament. *Studia psychologica*, ***37(3),*** 159-161.

Renuka, N & Anuradha, K. (2004). Psychosocial adjustment of school children with conduct problems. *The educational Review*, Bangalore, ***47(9)***, 3 -7.

Reynolds Shaw, Kathleen, A. (2006).A comparative study of adjustment to college of 1st generation and 2nd generation college students. *Dissertation Abstract International* , ***67(4)***, 1224-A.

Rice, K.G. (1992). Separation - individuation and adjustment to college: A longitudinal study. *Journal of Counselling Psychology,* ***39(2),*** 203-213.

Rice, K.G., Cole, D.A., & Lapsley, D.K. (1990). Separation-individuation, family cohesion and adjustment to college: Measurement validation and test of a theoretical model. *Journal of Counselling psychology*, ***37(2),*** 195-202.

Rice, K. G., & Whaley, T. J. (1994). A short-term longitudinal study of with in semester stability and change in attachment and college student adjustment. *Journal of College Student Development,* ***35(5)***, 324-330.

Rim, Y. (1989). Self-confrontation and Coping styles. *Personality & Individual differences,* ***10(9)***, 1011-1014.

Robbins, S. B., Lese, K. P., & Herrick, S. M. (1993). Interactions between goal instability and social support on college freshman adjustment. *Journal of Counselling and Development,* ***71(3)***, 343-348.

Robert W. Lent, Maria do Ceu Taveira, Hung-Bin Sheu &Daniel Singley (2008).Social cognitive predictors of academic adjustment and life satisfaction in Portuguese college students. *A longitudinal analysis-Online publication.*

Rosemary B. Closson & Wilma J. Henry (2008).The social adjustment of undergraduate white students in the minority on a Historically Black College Campus. *Journal of College Student Development,* ***49(6)***, 517-534.

Ruch, F.L. (1970). *Psychology and Life*. Bombay, India: D.B. Taraporewala Sons and Co.

Ryan, Allison, M & Shim, S. Serena (2008).An exploration of young adolescents' social achievement goals and social adjustment in middle school. *Journal of Educational Psychology,* ***100(3)***, 672-687.

Saklofske, D.H., & Kelly, I.W. (1995). Coping and personality. *Psychological Reports,* ***77(2)***, 481-482.

Schultheiss, D. E., Palladine., & Blustein, D.L. (1994). Role of adolescent -parent relationships in College student development and adjustment. *Journal of Counselling Psychology,* ***41(2)***, 248-255.

Schwitzer, A. M., McGovern, T.V., & Robbins, S.B. (1991). Adjustment out comes of a freshman seminar: A utilization focused approach. *Journal of College Student Development,* ***32(6)***, 484-489.

Schwitzer, A.M., Robbins, S.B., & McGovern, T.V. (1993). Influences of goal instability and social support on college adjustment. *Journal of College Student Development,* ***34(1)***, 21-25.

Shaffer, G. W., & Lazarus, R.S. (1952). *Fundamental Concepts in Clinical Psychology.* New York: McGraw-Hill.

Shaffer, L.F., & Shoben, E.J. (1956). *The psychology of adjustment.* Boston: Houghton Mifflin Co.

Shaffer, L.S. (1961). *Foundations of psychology* (Ed. p: 511). New York: Boring, Longfield and weld, John Willey & Sons.

Sharma, C.P. (1972). *Manual for personality adjustment Inventory*, (p: 1). Agra, India: Agra psychological Research Cell.

Sharma, K., Verma, B.P., & Kumar, R. (1989). The relationship of achievement motivation, adjustment and self-concept with academic performance of the students at +2 stage. *The progress of Education,* ***2,*** 30-32.

Sia, Ah-Hiok (2000). International students and their social net working process in adjusting to the new environment. A case study on the international students at the University of Missouri-Kansas city. *Dissertation Abstract International,* ***61(9)***, 3492A.

Silverthorn, N. A., & Gekoski, W. L. (1995). Social desirability effects on measures of adjustment to University, Independence from parents, and self-efficacy. *Journal of Clinical Psychology,* ***51(2),*** 244-251.

Singh, R.S. (1992). Student activism in relation to adjustment: A socio-psychological study. *Indian Psychological Review,* ***38(6-7)***, 1-5.

Smith, H. C. (1961). *Personality adjustment.* New York: McGraw-Hill Book Co.

Smith, M. A., & Baker, R. W. (1987). Freshman decidedness regarding academic major and adjustment to college. *Psychological Reports,* ***61(3),*** 847-853.

Sood, R. (1992). Academic achievement in relation to adjustment. *Journal of Psychological Research,* ***36(1)***, 1-4.

Srivastava,D.N & Govind Tiwari.(1986).*Adjustment Inventory* (For college students),Agra psychological Research Cell, Tiwari Kothi, Belangang, Agra.

Strange, A.A. (1998). Family context variables and the development of self-regulation in college students. *Adolescence,* ***33(129)***, 17-31.

Street, S., & Kromrey, J. D. (1994). Differences in adjustment issues for male and female adolescents. *Special services in the schools,* ***8(2),*** 143-154.

Stuart Marcia Ciscely (2002). An investigation of locus of control, psychological adjustment and Adjustment to College among international students from the Caribbean enrolled at a private historically black University, *Dissertation Abstract International,* ***61(8)***, 3071.

Sujatha., S., Gaonkar, V., Khadi, P., & Katarki, P.A. (1993). Factors influencing adjustment among adolescents. *Indian Psychological Review,* ***40(1-2),*** 35-40.

Swami, P.M. (1993). The adjustment of orphan students in comparison with normal students. *The progress of Education,* ***6,*** 125-128.

Takahashi, K., & Majima, N. (1994). Transition from home to college dormitory: The role of pre-established affective relationships in adjustment to a new life. *Journal of Research on Adolescence,* ***4(3),*** 367-384.

Tallent, N. (1978). *Psychology of adjustment: Understanding ourselves and others* (p: 2). New York: D.Van Nostrand Company.

Tanaka, T., Takai, J., Kohyama, T., & Fujihara, T. (1994). Adjustment patterns of international students in Japan. *International Journal of Intercultural Relations,* ***18(1),*** 55-75.

Terry, D.J. (1994). Determinants of coping: The role of stable and situational factors. *Journal of personality & social psychology,* ***66(5),*** 895-910.

Thorpe, L.P., & Schmuller, A.M. (1965). *Personality: An Interdisciplinary Approach.* New Delhi: D.Van Nostrand Company, Inc. New York, Affiliated East-West Press Pvt. Ltd.

Tiwari, S., & Pooranchand, L.J. (1994). A study of adjustment among high and low achieving adolescents. *Asian Journal of Psychological Education,* ***27(5-6),*** 28-29.

Tloczynski, J. (1994). A preliminary study of opening-up meditation college adjustment and self-actualization. *Psychological Reports,* ***75(1 pt 2),*** 449-450.

Tobacyk, J.J., & Driggers, E.C. (1989). Self-monitoring as a moderator of relationships between traditional religious belief and personality adjustment. *Psychological Reports, **65(3, pt 2)**,* 1185-1186.

Valentiner, D.P., Holahan, C. J., & Moos, R.H. (1994). Social supports, appraisals of event controllability and coping: An Integrative model. *Journal of Personality & Social psychology, **66(6)**,* 1094-1102.

Vanita Singh & Neeru Jasuja (2001). Comparison of cable TV viewers and non-viewers on adjustment, leisure time activities and scholastic achievement. *The Educational Review*, ***107(2)***, 12-14.

Verma, B.P., & Swain, B.C. (1991). Self-concept of adolescent students as a determinant of their personality adjustment. *The progress of Education, **1**,* 5-9.

Vonhaller, G.B. (1970). *Psychology* (p: 426). New York: Harper International Edition.

Vonhaller, Geuner, B., (1970).*Psychology*, New York: Houghton International, p-426.

Wang, Jing (2003). A study of the adjustment of international graduate students at American Universities including both resilience characteristics and traditional background factors. *Dissertation Abstract International*, ***64 (10)***, 3616.

Warren, Howard, C., (1934).*Dictionary of Education*, Boston: Houghton, p, 6.

Webster, A. Merrian (1951).*Webster's New Collegiate Dictionary*, London: G-Bell & Sons, p-12.

Weiss, L.H., & Schwarz, J.C. (1996). The relationship between parenting types and older adolescents' personality, academic achievement, adjustment and substance use. *Child Development, **67(5)**,* 2101-2114.

Ying, Yu-Wen & Han, Meekyun (2008).Variation in the prediction of cross-cultural adjustment by ethnic density of longitudinal study of Taiwanese students in the United States. *College student Journal, **42(4)**,* 1075-1086.

Zakahi, W.R., Jordan, F.F., & Christopher, D. (1993). Social adjustment to college: Communication apprehension and social network development among college students. *Communication Research Reports, **10(1)**,* 39-46.

[illegible] moderators of relationships [illegible] and [illegible] [illegible].

[illegible] Interpersonal [illegible] [illegible].

[illegible] comparison of [illegible] TV [illegible].

[illegible] determination of their [illegible].

[illegible] International [illegible].

[illegible] International [illegible].

[illegible] A review of [illegible] and [illegible].

Warren, Howard [illegible].

[illegible] Cassel & [illegible].

[illegible] Sciences [illegible].

[illegible] Tribal [illegible].

[illegible]

Index

A

Academic factors, 34-37
Adjustment, 2
Adjustment dimensions, 92
  comparison across
    age, 93, 125
    branch, 126
    branch, 95, 127-128
    district, 98-99
    educational qualifications, 93-95\, 125-126
    marital status, 93, 125
    medium, 126, 95-96
    monthly family income, 103-104, 129-130
    native area, 127, 97-98
    parental education, 101-102, 128
    parental professions, 103, 129
    present stay, 99-101, 128
    sex, 93, 124-125
    social status, 96-97, 127
    teaching parents, 102, 128-129
    type of family, 104-105, 130
Adjustment of prospective teachers, 147
Agra Psychological Research Cell, 141
Ambedkar, B.R., 14
ANOVA, 23, 91

B

Bajpai, 75
Bengal Youth Adjustment Analyzer, 67
Branch and gender, 131-132

C

Caste, 146
Correlational analyses, 123, 136
  inter correlation matrix of adjustment dimensions, 123, 136-137
Cultural Distance Questionnaires, 45
Customs and traditions, 146

D

Darwin, 2
Democratic, 63
Discussion, 124-138

E

Emotional adjustment, 81, 84
Emotional factors, 33-34

F

Findings, 141

H

Health adjustment, 81, 86

Home adjustment, 81, 82

I

Indian adaptation of bell adjustment inventory, 140

Indian Education, 26

Integrated Tribal Development Authority (ITDA), 75

Interaction effects, 106, 130

age and gender, 130

branch and gender, 131-132

district and gender, 133

educational qualifications and gender, 131

interaction of

age and gender, 106

branch and gender, 108-109

district and gender, 113

educational qualifications and gender, 107-108

marital status and gender, 106-107

medium and gender, 109-111

monthly family income and gender, 122

native area and gender, 113

parental education and gender, 116

– professions and gender, 116-122

present stay and gender, 113-116

social status and gender, 111-113

teaching parents and gender, 116

type of family and gender, 122

marital status and gender, 131

medium and gender, 132

monthly family income and gender, 135

native area and gender, 133

parental education and gender, 134

– professions and gender, 135

present stay and gender, 133-134

social status and gender, 132

teaching parents and gender, 134

type of family and gender, 135-136

Introduction, 1-17

adjustment as relatedness, 5-6

– in social aspect, 6-7

characteristics of a well adjusted person, 12-13

definitions of adjustment, 7-9

environmental adjustment, 10-11

healthy personality as adjustment, 9-10

history of the word adjustment, 1-3

meaning of adjustment, 3

need of the study, 13-17

process of adjustment, 3-5

J

Jawahar Navodaya Vidyalaya, 22

K

Kinthala kalinga, 75
Kumar Revised Adjustment Inventory, 67

L

Literacy, 146

M

MANOVA, 40, 91
Maudsley Personality Inventory, 45
Methodology, 66-91
adjustment inventory, 67-68
– variables, 81
administration of the questionnaires, 88
age, 71
analysis of data, 90-91
branch, 72-73
data collection, 88
district, 76-77
educational qualifications, 72
hypotheses, 66
Indian adaptation of bell adjustment inventory, 68-69
individual variables, 69
language of the questionnaire, 88-89
marital status, 71-72
medium, 74
monthly family income, 79-81
native area, 75-76
objectives of the study, 66
parental education, 78
– professions, 79
present stay, 77-78
research tools used, 67
sample, 89
scoring of Indian adaptation of bell adjustment inventory, 90
– – the adjustment inventory, 89-90
– – the tests, 89
sex, 69-70
social status, 74-75
teaching parents, 78-79
type of family, 81
variables measured, 69
Mittal Adjustment Inventory, 67

N

Navodaya Vidayalayas, 24
NGC (National green crops), 146

P

Paderu, 75

R

Recommendations, 145
Region, 146
Religion, 146
Results, 92-123
Review of literature, 18-65
adjustment and
academic factors, 34-37
age, 20
attendance, 53
branch, 21-22
culture, 41-43
drinking behaviour, 59-60
economic status, 26-28
emotional factors, 33-34
environmental factors, 38-40

family relationships, 47-49
foreign culture, 43-47
gender, 18-20
health factors, 37-38
marital status, 20-21
medium, 22-23
native areas, 24-25
other studies, 60-65
parental attachment, 49-51
parental conflicts, 52-53
personality factors, 53-56
present stay, 25-26
psychopathology, 56-59
social factors, 28-33
social status, 23
training programmes, 40-41

Anderson, 33
Anuradha, 24
Bajpai, 23
Campbell, 45
Chaudhury, 47
Christopher, 30
Doughlas, 42
Elizabeth, Carter, 21
Floyd, 25
Furukawa, 43
Hadley, 64
Heather, 32
Henning, 63
Kasinath, 22
Kelly, Warren, 64
Khan, 27
Kiefer, 31
Krishna, 27
Lakshmi, 19
Lecci, 61
Mishra, 28
Patrycia, 42
Rahmeen, Abdul, 28
Rajan, 22
Rao, Bhaskar, 19
Ray, 36
Rice, 60
Robert, W. Lent, 35
Ryan, 31
Schwitzer, 29
Smith, 34
Sood, 36
Swami, 19
Tanaka, 43
Taylor, 54
Tiwari, 37
Verma, 36

S

Saxena Adjustment Inventory, 67
SC, 74, 127
Social adjustment, 81, 82
Srikakulam, 14, 17, 88
ST, 74, 127
Suggestions, 146

T

Total adjustment, 81, 87

U

United States, 45
University Departments of Psychology, 13

V

Vilnius University in Lithuania, 56
Visakhapatnam, 88
Vizianagaram, 14, 17, 75, 88, 141

❑❑❑